Eggcellent Eats

Macaroni, Omelette, and Cheese Creations

By

Anita T. Walker

MACARONI.

MACARONI Á LA ITALIENNE.

Divide a quarter of a pound of macaroni into four-inch pieces. Simmer fifteen minutes in plenty of boiling water, salted. Drain. Put the macaroni into a saucepan and turn over it a strong soup stock, enough to prevent burning. Strew over it an ounce of grated cheese; when the cheese is melted, dish. Put alternate layers of macaroni and cheese, then turn over the soup stock and bake half an hour.

MACARONI AND CHEESE.

Break half a pound of macaroni into pieces an inch or two long; cook it in boiling water, enough to cover it well; put in a good teaspoonful of salt; let it boil about twenty minutes. Drain it well and then put a layer in the bottom of a well-buttered pudding-dish; upon this some grated cheese and small pieces of butter, a bit of salt, then more macaroni, and so on, filling the dish; sprinkle the top layer with a thick layer of cracker crumbs. Pour over the whole a teacupful of cream or milk. Set it in the oven and bake half an hour. It should be nicely browned on top. Serve in the same dish in which it was baked with a clean napkin pinned around it.

TIMBALE OF MACARONI.

Break in very short lengths small macaroni (vermicelli, spaghetti, tagliarini). Let it be rather overdone; dress it with butter and grated cheese; then work into it one or two eggs, according to quantity. Butter and bread crumb a plain mold, and when the macaroni is nearly cold fill the mold with it, pressing it well down and leaving a hollow in the centre, into which place a well-flavored mince of meat, poultry or game; then fill up the mold with more macaroni, pressed well down. Bake in a moderately heated oven, turn out and serve.

MACARONI Á LA CRÊME.

Boil one-quarter of a pound of macaroni in plenty of hot water, salted, until tender; put half a pint of milk in a double boiler, and when it boils stir into it a mixture of two tablespoonfuls of butter and one of flour. Add two tablespoonfuls of cream, a little white and cayenne pepper; salt to taste, and from one-quarter to one-half a pound of grated cheese, according to taste. Drain and dish the macaroni; pour the boiling sauce over it and serve immediately.

MACARONI AND TOMATO SAUCE.

Divide half a pound of macaroni into four-inch pieces, put it into boiling salted water enough to cover it; boil from fifteen to twenty minutes then drain; arrange it neatly on a hot dish and pour tomato sauce over it, and serve immediately while hot. See SAUCES for tomato sauce.

BUTTER AND CHEESE

TO MAKE BUTTER.

Thoroughly scald the churn, then cool well with ice or spring water. Now pour in the thick cream; churn fast at first, then, as the butter forms, more slowly; always with perfect regularity; in warm weather, pour a little cold water into the churn, should the butter form slowly; in the winter, if the cream is too cold, add a little warm water to bring it to the proper temperature. When the butter has "come", rinse the sides of the churn down with cold water and take the butter up with a perforated dasher or a wooden ladle, turning it dexterously just below the surface of the buttermilk to catch every stray bit; have ready some very cold water in a deep wooden tray; and into this plunge the dasher when you draw it from the churn; the butter will float off, leaving the dasher free. When you have collected all the butter, gather behind a wooden butter ladle and drain off the water, squeezing and pressing the butter with the ladle; then pour on more cold water and work the butter with the ladle to get the milk out, drain off the water, sprinkle salt over the butter—a tablespoonful to a pound; work it in a little and set in a cool place for an hour to harden, then work and knead it until not another drop of water exudes, and the butter is perfectly smooth, and close in texture and polish; then with the ladle make up into rolls, little balls, stamped pats, etc.

The churn, dasher, tray and ladle should be well scalded before using, so that the butter will not stick to them, and then cooled with very cold water.

When you skim cream into your cream jar, stir it well into what is already there, so that it may all sour alike; and no *fresh cream should be put with it* within twelve hours before churning, or the butter will not come quickly; and perhaps, not at all.

Butter is indispensable in almost all culinary preparations. Good fresh butter, used in moderation, is easily digested; it is softening, nutritious and fattening, and is far more easily digested than any other of the oleaginous substances sometimes used in its place.

TO MAKE BUTTER QUICKLY.

Immediately after the cow is milked, strain the milk into clean pans, and set it over a moderate fire until it is scalding hot; do not let it boil; then set it aside; when it is cold, skim off the cream; the milk will still be fit for any ordinary use; when you have enough cream put it into a clean earthen basin; beat it with a wooden spoon until the butter is made, which will not be long; then take it from the milk and work it with a little cold water, until it is free from milk; then drain off the water, put a small tablespoonful of fine salt to each pound of butter and work it in. A small teaspoonful of fine white sugar, worked in with the salt, will be found an improvement—sugar is a great preservative. Make the butter in a roll; cover it with a bit of muslin and keep it in a cool place. A reliable recipe.

A BRINE TO PRESERVE BUTTER.

First work your butter into small rolls, wrapping each one carefully in a clean muslin cloth, tying them up with a string. Make a brine, say three gallons, having it strong enough of salt to bear up an egg; add half a teacupful of pure, white sugar, and one tablespoonful of saltpetre; boil the brine, and when cold strain it carefully. Pour it over the rolls so as to more than cover them, as this excludes the air. Place a weight over all to keep the rolls under the surface.

PUTTING UP BUTTER TO KEEP.

Take of the best pure common salt two quarts, one ounce of white sugar and one of saltpetre; pulverize them together completely. Work the butter well, then thoroughly work in an ounce of this mixture to every pound of butter. The butter is to be made into half-pound rolls, and put into the following brine—to three gallons of brine strong enough to bear an egg, add a quarter of a pound of white sugar.

Orange Co., N. Y. Style

CURDS AND CREAM.

One gallon of milk will make a moderate dish. Put one spoonful of prepared rennet to each quart of milk, and when you find that it has become curd, tie it loosely in a thin cloth and hang it to drain; do not wring or press the cloth; when drained, put the curd into a mug and set in cool water, which must be frequently changed (a refrigerator saves this trouble). When you dish it, if there is whey in the mug, lie it gently out without pressing the curd; lay it on a deep dish, and pour fresh cream over it; have powdered loaf-sugar to eat with it; also hand the nutmeg grater.

Prepared rennet can be had at almost any druggist's, and at a reasonable price.

NEW JERSEY CREAM CHEESE.

First scald the quantity of milk desired; let it cool a little, then add the rennet; the directions for quantity are given on the packages of "Prepared Rennet." When the curd is formed, take it out on a ladle without breaking it; lay it on a thin cloth held by two persons; dash a ladleful of water over each ladleful of curd, to separate the curd; hang it up to drain the water off, and then put it under a light press for one hour; cut the curd with a thread into small pieces; lay a cloth between each two, and press for an hour; take them out, rub them with fine salt, let them lie on a board for an hour, and wash them in cold water; let them lie to drain, and in a day or two the skin will look dry; put some sweet grass under and over them, and they will soon ripen.

COTTAGE CHEESE.

Put a pan of sour or loppered milk on the stove or range where it is not too hot; let it scald until the whey rises to the top (be careful that it does not boil, or the curd will become hard and tough). Place a clean doth or towel over a sieve and pour this whey and curd into it, living it covered to drain two or three hours; then put it into a dish and chop it fine with a spoon, adding a teaspoonful of salt, a tablespoonful of butter and enough sweet cream to make the cheese the consistency of putty. With your hands make it into little balls flattened. Keep it in a cool place. Many like it made rather thin with cream, serving it in a deep dish. You may make this cheese of sweet milk by forming the curd with prepared rennet.

SLIP.

Slip is bonny-clabber without its acidity, and so delicate is its flavor that many persons like it just as well as ice cream. It is prepared thus:—Make a quart of milk moderately warm; then stir into it one large spoonful of the preparation called rennet; set it by, and when cool again it will be as stiff as jelly. It should be made only a few hours before it is to be used, or it will be tough and watery; in summer set the dish on ice after it has jellied. It must be served with powdered sugar, nutmeg and cream.

CHEESE FONDU.

Melt an ounce of butter and whisk into it a pint of boiled milk. Dissolve two tablespoonfuls of flour in a gill of cold milk, add it to the boiled milk and let it cool. Beat the yolks of four eggs with a heaping teaspoonful of salt, half a teaspoonful of pepper and five ounces of grated cheese. Whip the whites of the eggs and add them, pour the mixture into a deep tin lined with buttered paper, and allow for the rising, say four inches. Bake twenty minutes and serve the moment it leaves the oven.

CHEESE SOUFFLÉ.

Melt an ounce of butter in a saucepan; mix smoothly with it one ounce of flour, a pinch of salt and cayenne and a quarter of a pint of milk; simmer the mixture gently over the fire, stirring it all the time, till it is as thick as melted butter, stir into it about three ounces of finely-grated parmesan, or any good cheese. Turn it into a basin and mix with it the yolks of two well-beaten eggs. Whisk three whites to a solid froth, and just before the souffle is baked put them into it, and pour the mixture into a small round tin. It should be only half filled, as the fondu will rise very high. Pin a napkin around the dish in which it is baked, and serve the moment it is baked. It would be well to have a metal cover strongly heated. Time twenty minutes. Sufficient for six persons.

SCALLOPED CHEESE.

Any person who is fond of cheese could not fail to favor this recipe.

Take three slices of bread well-buttered, first cutting off the brown outside crust. Grate fine a quarter of a pound of any kind of good cheese; lay the bread in layers in a buttered baking-dish, sprinkle over it the grated cheese, some salt and pepper to taste. Mix four well-beaten eggs with three cups of milk; pour it over the bread and cheese. Bake it in a hot oven as you would cook a bread pudding. This makes an ample dish for four people.

PASTRY RAMAKINS.

Take the remains or odd pieces of any light puff paste left from pies or tarts; gather up the pieces of paste, roll it out evenly, and sprinkle it with grated cheese of a nice flavor. Fold the paste in three, roll it out again, and sprinkle more cheese over; fold the paste, roll it out, and with a paste-cutter shape it in any way that may be desired. Bake the ramakins in a brisk oven from ten to fifteen minutes; dish them on a hot napkin and serve quickly. The appearance of this dish may be very much improved by brushing the ramakins over with yolk of egg before they are placed in the oven. Where expense is not objected to, parmesan is the best kind of cheese to use for making this dish.

Very nice with a cup of coffee for a lunch.

CAYENNE CHEESE STRAWS.

A quarter of a pound of flour, two ounces butter, two ounces grated parmesan cheese, a pinch of salt and a few grains of cayenne pepper. Mix into a paste with the yolk of an egg. Roll out to the thickness of a silver quarter, about four or five inches long; cut into strips about a third of an inch wide, twist them as you would a paper spill and lay them on a baking-sheet slightly floured. Bake in a moderate oven until crisp, but they must not be the least brown. If put away in a tin these straws will keep a long time. Serve cold, piled tastefully on a glass dish. You can make the straws of remnants of puff pastry, rolling in the grated cheese.

CHEESE CREAM TOAST.

Stale bread may be served as follows: Toast the slices and cover them slightly with grated cheese; make a cream for ten slices out of a pint of milk and two tablespoonfuls of plain flour. The milk should be boiling, and the flour mixed in a little cold water before stirring in. When the cream is nicely cooked, season with salt and butter; set the toast and cheese in the oven for three or four minutes and then pour the cream over them.

WELSH RAREBIT.

Grate three ounces of dry cheese and mix it with the yolks of two eggs, put four ounces of grated bread and three of butter; beat the whole together in a mortar with a dessertspoonful of made mustard, a little salt and some pepper; toast some slices of bread, cut off the outside crust, cut it in shapes and spread the paste thick upon them, and put them in the oven, let them become hot and slightly browned, serve hot as possible.

EGGS AND OMELETS.

There are so many ways of cooking and dressing eggs, that it seems unnecessary for the ordinary family to use those that are not the most practical.

To ascertain the freshness of an egg, hold it between your thumb and forefinger in a horizontal position, with a strong light in front of you. The fresh egg will have a clear appearance, both upper and lower sides being the same. The stale egg will have a clear appearance at the lower side, while the upper side will exhibit a dark or cloudy appearance.

Another test is to put them in a pan of cold water; those that are the first to sink are the freshest; the stale will rise and float on top; or, if the large end turns up in the water, they are not fresh. The best time for preserving eggs is from July to September.

TO PRESERVE EGGS.

There are several recipes for preserving eggs and we give first one which we know to be effectual, keeping them fresh from August until Spring. Take a piece of quick-lime as large as a good-sized lemon and two teacupfuls of salt; put it into a large vessel and slack it with a gallon of boiling water. It will boil and bubble until thick as cream; when it is cold, pour off the top, which will be perfectly clear. Drain off this liquor, and pour it over your eggs; see that the liquor more than covers them. A stone jar is the most convenient—one that holds about six quarts.

Another manner of preserving eggs is to pack them in a jar with layers of salt between, the large end of the egg downward, with a thick layer of salt at the top; cover tightly and set in a cool place.

Some put them in a wire basket or a piece of mosquito net and dip them in boiling water half a minute; then pack in sawdust. Still another manner is to dissolve a cheap article of gum arabic, about as thin as muscilage, and brush over each egg with it; then pack in powdered charcoal; set in a cool, dark place.

Eggs can be kept for some time by smearing the shells with butter or lard; then packed in plenty of bran or sawdust, the eggs not allowed to touch one another; or coat the eggs with melted paraffine.

BOILED EGGS.

Eggs for boiling cannot be too fresh, or boiled too soon after they are laid; but rather a longer time should be allowed for boiling a new-laid egg than for one that is three or four days old. Have ready a saucepan of boiling water; put the eggs into it gently with a spoon, letting the spoon touch the bottom of the saucepan before it is withdrawn, that the egg may not fall and consequently crack. For those who like eggs lightly boiled, three minutes will be found sufficient; three and three-quarters to four minutes will be ample time to set the white nicely; and if liked hard, six or seven minutes will not be found too long. Should the eggs be unusually large, as those of black Spanish fowls sometimes are, allow an extra half minute for them. Eggs for salad should be boiled for ten or fifteen minutes, and should be placed in a basin of cold water for a few minutes to shrink the meat from the shell; they should then be rolled on the table with the hand and the shell will peel off easily.

SOFT BOILED EGGS.

When properly cooked eggs are done evenly through, like any other food. This result may be obtained by putting the eggs into a dish with a cover, or a tin pail, and then pouring upon them *boiling* water—two quarts or more to a dozen of eggs—and cover and set them away where they will keep *hot* and *not* boil for ten to twelve minutes. The heat of the water cooks the eggs slowly, evenly and sufficiently, leaving the centre or yolk harder than the white, and the egg tastes as much richer and nicer as a fresh egg is nicer than a stale egg.

SCALLOPED EGGS.

Hard-boil twelve eggs; slice them thin in rings; in the bottom of a large well-buttered baking-dish place a layer of grated bread crumbs, then one of eggs; cover with bits of butter and sprinkle with pepper and salt. Continue thus to blend these ingredients until the dish is full; be sure, though, that the crumbs cover the eggs upon top. Over the whole pour a large teacupful of sweet cream or milk and brown nicely in a moderately heated oven.

SHIRRED EGGS.

Set into the oven until quite hot a common white dish large enough to hold the number of eggs to be cooked, allowing plenty of room for each. Melt in it a small piece of butter, and breaking the eggs carefully in a saucer, one at a time, slip them into the hot dish; sprinkle over them a small quantity of pepper and salt and allow them to cook four or five minutes. Adding a tablespoonful of cream for every two eggs, when the eggs are first slipped in, is a great improvement.

This is far more delicate than fried eggs.

Or prepare the eggs the same and set them in a steamer over boiling water.

They are usually served in hotels baked in individual dishes, about two in a dish, and in the same dish they were baked in.

SCRAMBLED EGGS.

Put a tablespoonful of butter into a hot frying pan; tip around so that it will touch all sides of the pan. Having ready half a dozen eggs broken in a dish, salted and peppered, turn them (without beating) into the hot butter; stir them one way briskly for five or six minutes or until they are mixed. Be careful that they do not get too hard. Turn over toast or dish up without.

POACHED OR DROPPED EGGS.

Have one quart of *boiling* water and one tablespoonful of salt in a frying pan. Break the eggs, one by one, into a saucer, and slide carefully into the salted water. Dash with a spoon a little water over the egg, to keep the top white.

The beauty of a poached egg is for the yolk to be seen blushing through the white, which should only be just sufficiently hardened to form a transparent veil for the egg.

Cook until the white is firm, and lift out with a griddle cake turner and place on toasted bread. Serve immediately.

A tablespoonful of vinegar put into the water keeps the eggs from spreading.

Open gem rings are nice placed in the water and an egg dropped into each ring.

FRIED EGGS.

Break the eggs, one at a time, into a saucer, and then slide them carefully off into a frying pan of lard and butter mixed, dipping over the eggs the hot grease in spoonfuls, or turn them over, frying both sides without breaking them. They require about three minutes' cooking.

Eggs can be fried round like balls, by dropping one at a time into a quantity of hot lard, the same as for fried cakes, first stirring the hot lard with a stick until it runs round like a whirlpool; this will make the eggs look like balls. Take out with a skimmer. Eggs can be poached the same in boiling water.

EGGS AUX FINES HERBES.

Roll an ounce of butter in a good teaspoonful of flour; season with pepper, salt and nutmeg; put it into a coffeecupful of fresh milk, together with two teaspoonfuls of chopped parsley; stir and simmer it for fifteen minutes, add a teacupful of thick cream. Hard-boil five eggs and halve them; arrange them in a dish with the ends upwards, pour the sauce over them, and decorate with little heaps of fried bread crumbs round the margin of the dish.

POACHED EGGS Á LA CRÊME.

Put a quart of hot water, a tablespoonful of vinegar and a teaspoonful of salt into a frying pan, and break each egg separately into a saucer; slip the egg carefully into the hot water, simmer three or four minutes until the white is set, then with a skimmer lift them out into a hot dish. Empty the pan of its contents, put in half a cup of cream, or rich milk; if milk, a large spoonful of butter; pepper and salt to taste, thicken with a very little cornstarch; let it boil up once, and turn it over the dish of poached eggs. It can be served on toast or without.

It is a better plan to warm the cream in butter in a separate dish, that the eggs may not have to stand.

EGGS IN CASES.

Make little paper cases of buttered writing paper; put a small piece of butter in each, and a little chopped parsley or onion, pepper and salt. Place the cases upon a gridiron over a moderate fire of bright coals, and when the butter melts, break a fresh egg into each case. Strew in upon them a few seasoned bread crumbs, and when nearly done, glaze the tops with a hot shovel. Serve in the paper cases.

MINCED EGGS.

Chop up four or five hard-boiled eggs; do not mince them too fine. Put over the fire in a suitable dish a cupful of milk, a tablespoonful of butter, salt and pepper, and some savory chopped small. When this comes to a boil stir into it a tablespoonful of flour, dissolved in a little cold milk. When it cooks thick like cream put in the minced eggs. Stir it gently around and around for a few moments and serve, garnished with sippets of toast. Any particular flavor may be given to this dish, such as that of mushrooms, truffles, catsup, essence of shrimps, etc., or some shred anchovy may be added to the mince.

MIXED EGGS AND BACON.

Take a nice rasher of mild bacon; cut it into squares no larger than dice; fry it quickly until nicely browned; but on no account burn it. Break half a dozen eggs into a basin, strain and season them with pepper, add them to the bacon, stir the whole about and, when sufficiently firm, turn it out into a dish. Decorate with hot pickles.

MIXED EGGS GENERALLY—SAVORY OR SWEET.

Much the same method is followed in mixed eggs generally, whatever may be added to them; really it is nothing more than an omelet which is stirred about in the pan while it is being dressed, instead of being allowed to set as a pancake. Chopped tongue, oysters, shrimps, sardines, dried salmon, anchovies, herbs, may be used.

COLD EGGS FOR A PICNIC.

This novel way of preparing cold egg for the lunch-basket fully repays one for the extra time required. Boil hard several eggs, halve them lengthwise; remove the yolks and chop them fine with cold chicken, lamb, veal or any tender, roasted meat; or with bread soaked in milk and any salad, as parsley, onion, celery, the bread being half of the whole; or with grated cheese, a little olive oil, drawn butter, flavored. Fill the cavity in the egg with either of these mixtures, or any similar preparation. Press the halves together, roll twice in beaten egg and bread crumbs, and dip into boiling lard. When the color rises delicately, drain them and they are ready for use.

OMELETS.

In making an omelet, care should be taken that the omelet pan is hot and dry. To insure this, put a small quantity of lard or suet into a clean frying pan, let it simmer a few minutes, then remove it; wipe the pan dry with a towel, and then put in a tablespoonful of butter. The smoothness of the pan is most essential, as the least particle of roughness will cause the omelet to stick. As a general rule, a small omelet can be made more successfully than a large one, it being much better to make two small ones of four eggs each, than to try double the number of eggs in one omelet and fail. Allow one egg to a person in making an omelet and one tablespoonful of milk; this makes an omelet more puffy and tender than one made without milk. Many prefer them without milk.

Omelets are called by the name of what is added to give them flavor, as minced ham, salmon, onions, oysters, etc., beaten up in the eggs in due quantity, which gives as many different kind of omelets.

They are also served over many kinds of thick sauces or purees, such as tomato, spinach, endive, lettuce, celery, etc.

If vegetables are to be added, they should be already cooked, seasoned and hot; place in the centre of the omelet, just before turning; so with mushroom, shrimps, or any cooked ingredients. All omelets should be served the moment they are done, as they harden by standing, and care taken that they do not *cook too much.*

Sweet omelets are generally used for breakfast or plain desserts.

PLAIN OMELET.

Put a smooth, clean, iron frying pan on the fire to heat; meanwhile, beat four eggs very light, the whites to a stiff froth and the yolks to a thick batter. Add to the yolks four tablespoonfuls of milk, pepper and salt; and, lastly, stir in the whites lightly. Put a piece of butter nearly half the size of an egg into the heated pan; turn it so that it will moisten the entire bottom, taking care that it does not scorch. Just as it begins to boil, pour in the eggs. Hold the frying pan handle in your left hand, and, as the eggs whiten, carefully, with a spoon, draw up lightly from the bottom, letting the raw part run out on the pan, till all be equally cooked; shake with your left hand, till the omelet be free from the pan, then turn with a spoon one half of the omelet over the other; let it remain a moment, but continue shaking, lest it adhere; toss to a warm platter held in the right hand, or lift with a flat, broad shovel; the omelet will be firm around the edge, but creamy and light inside.

MEAT OR FISH OMELETS.

Take cold meat, fish, game or poultry of any kind; remove all skin, sinew, etc., and either cut it small or pound it to a paste in a mortar, together with a proper proportion of spices and salt; then either toss it in a buttered frying pan over a clear fire till it begins to brown and pour beaten eggs upon it, or beat it up with the eggs, or spread it upon them after they have begun to set in the pan. In any case serve hot, with or without a sauce, but garnish with crisp herbs in branches, pickles, or sliced lemon. The right proportion is one tablespoonful of meat to four eggs. A little milk, gravy, water, or white wine, may be advantageously added to the eggs while they are being beaten.

Potted meats make admirable omelets in the above manner.

VEGETABLE OMELET.

Make a purée by mashing up ready-dressed vegetables, together with a little milk, cream or gravy and some seasoning. The most suitable vegetables are cucumbers, artichokes, onions, sorrel, green peas, tomatoes, lentils, mushrooms, asparagus tops, potatoes, truffles or turnips. Prepare some eggs by beating them very light. Pour them into a nice hot frying pan, containing a spoonful of butter; spread the purée upon the upper side; and when perfectly hot, turn or fold the omelet together and serve. Or cold vegetables may be merely chopped small, then tossed in a little butter, and some beaten and seasoned eggs poured over.

OMELET OF HERBS.

Parsley, thyme and sweet marjoram mixed gives the famous *omelette aux fines herbes* so popular at every wayside inn in the most remote corner of sunny France. An omelet "jardiniere" is two tablespoonfuls of mixed parsley, onion, chives, shallots and a few leaves each of sorrel and chevril, minced fine and stirred into the beaten eggs before cooking. It will take a little more butter to fry it than a plain one.

CHEESE OMELET.

Beat up three eggs, and add to them a tablespoonful of milk and a tablespoonful of grated cheese; add a little more cheese before folding; turn it out on a hot dish; grate a little cheese over it before serving.

ASPARAGUS OMELET.

Boil with a little salt, and until about half cooked, eight or ten stalks of asparagus, and cut the eatable part into rather small pieces; beat the egg and mix the asparagus with them. Make the omelet as above directed. Omelet with parsley is made by adding a little chopped parsley.

TOMATO OMELET. No. 1.

Peel a couple of tomatoes, which split into four pieces; remove the seeds and cut them into small dice; then fry them with a little butter until nearly done, adding salt and pepper. Beat the eggs and mix the tomatoes with them, and make the omelet as usual. Or stew a few tomatoes in the usual way and spread over before folding.

TOMATO OMELET. No. 2.

Cut in slices and place in a stewpan six peeled tomatoes; add a tablespoonful of cold water, a little pepper and salt. When they begin to simmer, break in six eggs, stir well, stirring one way, until the eggs are cooked, but not too hard. Serve warm.

RICE OMELET.

Take a cup of cold boiled rice, turn over it a cupful of warm milk, add a tablespoonful of butter melted, a level teaspoonful of salt, a dash of pepper; mix well, then add three well-beaten eggs. Put a tablespoonful of butter in a hot frying pan, and when it begins to boil pour in the omelet and set the pan in a hot oven. As soon as it is cooked through, fold it double, turn it out on a hot dish, and serve at once. Very good.

HAM OMELET.

Cut raw ham into dice, fry with butter and when cooked enough, turn the beaten egg over it and cook as a plain omelet.

If boiled ham is used, mince it and mix with the egg after they are beaten. Bacon may be used instead of raw ham.

CHICKEN OMELET.

Mince rather fine one cupful of cooked chicken, warm in a teacupful of cream or rich milk a tablespoonful of butter, salt and pepper; thicken with a large tablespoonful of flour. Make a plain omelet, then add this mixture just before turning it over. This is much better than the dry minced chicken. Tongue is equally good.

MUSHROOM OMELET.

Clean a cupful of large button mushrooms, canned ones may be used; cut them into bits. Put into a stewpan an ounce of butter and let it melt; add the mushrooms, a teaspoonful of salt, half a teaspoonful of pepper and half a cupful of cream or milk. Stir in a teaspoonful of flour, dissolved in a little milk or water to thicken, if needed. Boil ten minutes, and set aside until the omelet is ready.

Make a plain omelet the usual way, and just before doubling it, turn the mushrooms over the centre and serve hot.

OYSTER OMELET.

Parboil a dozen oysters in their own liquor, skim them out and let them cool; add them to the beaten eggs, either whole or minced. Cook the same as a plain omelet.

Thicken the liquid with butter rolled in flour; season with salt, cayenne pepper and a teaspoonful of chopped parsley. Chop up the oysters and add to the sauce. Put a few spoonfuls in the centre of the omelet before folding; when dished, pour the remainder of the sauce around it.

FISH OMELET.

Make a plain omelet, and when ready to fold, spread over it fish prepared as follows: Add to a cupful of any kind of cold fish, broken fine, cream enough to moisten it, seasoned with a tablespoonful of butter; then pepper and salt to taste. Warm together.

ONION OMELET.

Make a plain omelet, and when ready to turn spread over it a teaspoonful each of chopped onion and minced parsley; then fold, or, if preferred, mix the minces into the eggs before cooking.

JELLY OMELET.

Make a plain omelet, and just before folding together, spread with some kind of jelly. Turn out on a warm platter. Dust it with powdered sugar.

BREAD OMELET. No. 1.

Break four eggs into a basin and carefully remove the treadles; have ready a tablespoonful of grated and sifted bread; soak it in either milk, water, cream, white wine, gravy, lemon juice, brandy or rum, according as the omelet is intended to be sweet or savory. Well beat the eggs together with a little nutmeg, pepper and salt; add the bread, and, beating constantly (or the omelet will be crumbly), get ready a frying pan, buttered and made thoroughly hot; put in the omelet; do it on one side only; turn it upon a dish, and fold it double to prevent the steam from condensing. Stale sponge-cake, grated biscuit, or pound cake, may replace the bread for a sweet omelet, when pounded loaf sugar should be sifted over it, and the dish decorated with lumps of currant jelly. This makes a nice dessert.

BREAD OMELET. No. 2.

Let one teacupful of milk come to a boil, pour it over one teacupful of bread crumbs and let it stand a few minutes. Break six eggs into a bowl, stir (not beat) till well mixed; then add the milk and bread, season with pepper and salt, mix all well together and turn into a hot frying pan, containing a large spoonful of butter boiling hot. Fry the omelet slowly, and when brown on the bottom cut in squares and turn again, fry to a delicate brown and serve hot.

Cracker omelet may be made by substituting three or four rolled crackers in place of bread.

BAKED OMELET.

Beat the whites and yolks of four or six eggs separately; add to the yolks a small cup of milk, a tablespoonful of flour or cornstarch, a teaspoonful of baking powder, one-half teaspoonful of salt, and, lastly, the stiff-beaten whites. Bake in a well-buttered pie-tin or plate about half an hour in a steady oven. It should be served the moment it is taken from the oven, as it is liable to fall.

OMELET SOUFFLÉ.

Break six eggs into separate cups; beat four of the yolks, mix with them one teaspoonful of flour, three tablespoonfuls of powdered sugar, very little salt. Flavor with extract lemon or any other of the flavors that may be preferred. Whisk the whites of six eggs to a firm froth; mix them lightly with the yolks; pour the mixture into a greased pan or dish; bake in a quick oven. When well-risen and lightly browned on the top, it is done; roll out in warm dish, sift pulverized sugar over, and send to table.

RUM OMELET.

Put a small quantity of lard into the pan; let it simmer a few minutes and remove it; wipe the pan dry with a towel, and put in a little fresh lard in which the omelet may be fried. Care should be taken that the lard does not burn, which would spoil the color of the omelet. Break three eggs separately; put them into a bowl and whisk them thoroughly with a fork. The longer they are beaten, the lighter will the omelet be. Beat up a teaspoonful of milk with the eggs and continue to beat until the last moment before pouring into the pan, which should be over a hot fire. As soon as the omelet sets, remove the pan from the hottest part of the fire. Slip a knife under it to prevent sticking to the pan. When the centre is almost firm, slant the pan, work the omelet in shape to fold easily find neatly, and when slightly browned, hold a platter against the edge of the pan and deftly turn it out on to the hot dish. Dust a liberal quantity of powdered sugar over it, and singe the sugar into neat stripes with a hot iron rod, heated in the coals; pour a glass of warm Jamaica rum around it, and when it is placed on the table set fire to the rum. With a tablespoon dash the burning rum over the omelet, put out the fire and serve. Salt *mixed* with the eggs prevents them from rising, and when it is so used the omelet will look flabby, yet without salt it will taste insipid.

SANDWICHES.

HAM SANDWICHES.

Make a dressing of half a cup of butter, one tablespoonful of mixed mustard, one of salad oil, a little red or white pepper, a pinch of salt and the yolk of an egg; rub the butter to a cream, add the other ingredients and mix thoroughly; then stir in as much chopped ham as will make it consistent and spread between thin slices of bread. Omit salad oil and substitute melted butter if preferred.

HAM SANDWICHES, PLAIN.

Trim the crusts from thin slices of bread; butter them and lay between every two some thin slices of cold boiled ham. Spread the meat with a little mustard if liked.

CHICKEN SANDWICHES.

Mince up fine any cold boiled or roasted chicken; put it into a saucepan with gravy, water or cream enough to soften it; add a good piece of butter, a pinch of pepper; work it very smooth while it is heating until it looks almost like a paste. Then spread it on a plate to cool. Spread it between slices of buttered bread.

SARDINE SANDWICHES.

Take two boxes of sardines and throw the contents into hot water, having first drained away all the oil. A few minutes will free the sardines from grease. Pour away the water and dry the fish in a cloth; then scrape away the skins and pound the sardines in a mortar till reduced to paste; add pepper, salt and some tiny pieces of lettuce, and spread on the sandwiches, which have been previously cut as above. The lettuce adds very much to the flavor of the sardines.

Or chop the sardines up fine and squeeze a few drops of lemon juice into them, and spread between buttered bread or cold biscuits.

WATER CRESS SANDWICHES.

Wash well some water cress and then dry them in a cloth, pressing out every atom of moisture as far as possible; then mix with the cress hard-boiled eggs chopped fine, and seasoned with salt and pepper. Have a stale loaf and some fresh butter, and with a sharp knife cut as many thin slices as will be required for two dozen sandwiches; then cut the cress into small pieces, removing the stems; place it between each slice of bread and butter, with a slight sprinkling of lemon juice; press down the slices hard, and cut them sharply on a board into small squares, leaving no crust.

Nantasket Beach.

EGG SANDWICHES.

Hard boil some very fresh eggs and when cold cut them into moderately thin slices and lay them between some bread and butter cut as thin as possible; season them with pepper, salt and nutmeg. For picnic parties, or when one is traveling, these sandwiches are far preferable to hard-boiled eggs *au naturel*.

MUSHROOM SANDWICHES.

Mince beef tongue and boiled mushrooms together, add French mustard and spread between buttered bread.

CHEESE SANDWICHES.

These are extremely nice and are very easily made. Take one hard-boiled egg, a quarter of a pound of common cheese grated, half a teaspoonful of salt, half a teaspoonful of pepper, half a teaspoonful of mustard, one tablespoonful of melted butter, and one tablespoonful of vinegar or cold water. Take the yolk of the egg and put it into a small bowl and crumble it down, put into it the butter and mix it smooth with a spoon, then add the salt, pepper, mustard and the cheese, mixing each well. Then put in the tablespoonful of vinegar, which will make it the proper thickness. If vinegar is not relished, then use cold water instead. Spread this between two biscuits or pieces of oat-cake, and you could not require a better sandwich. Some people will prefer the sandwiches less highly seasoned. In that case, season to taste.

BREAD.

Among all civilized people bread has become an article of food of the first necessity; and properly so, for it constitutes of itself a complete life sustainer, the gluten, starch and sugar which it contains representing ozotized and hydro-carbonated nutrients, and combining the sustaining powers of the animal and vegetable kingdoms in one product. As there is no one article of food that enters so largely into our daily fare as bread, so no degree of skill in preparing other articles can compensate for lack of knowledge in the art of making good, palatable and nutritious bread. A little earnest attention to the subject will enable any one to comprehend the theory, and then ordinary care in practice will make one familiar with the process.

GENERAL DIRECTIONS.

The first thing required for making wholesome bread is the utmost cleanliness; the next is the soundness and sweetness of all the ingredients used for it; and, in addition to these, there must be attention and care through the whole process.

Salt is always used in bread-making, not only on account of its flavor, which destroys the insipid raw state of the flour, but because it makes the dough rise better.

In mixing with milk, the milk should be boiled—not simply scalded, but heated to boiling over hot water—then set aside to cool before mixing. Simple heating will not prevent bread from turning sour in the rising, while boiling will act as a preventative. So the milk should be thoroughly scalded, and should be used when it is just blood warm.

Too small a proportion of yeast, or insufficient time allowed for the dough to rise, will cause the bread to be heavy.

The yeast must be good and fresh if the bread is to be digestible and nice. Stale yeast produces, instead of vinous fermentation, an acetous fermentation, which flavors the bread and makes it disagreeable. A poor, thin yeast produces an imperfect fermentation, the result being a heavy, unwholesome loaf.

If either the sponge or the dough be permitted to overwork itself—that is to say, if the mixing and kneading be neglected when it has reached the proper point for either—sour bread will probably be the consequence in warm weather, and bad bread in any. The goodness will also be endangered by placing it so near a fire as to make any part of it hot, instead of maintaining the gentle and equal degree of heat required for its due fermentation.

Heavy bread will also most likely be the result of making the dough very hard and letting it become quite cold, particularly in winter.

An almost certain way of spoiling dough is to leave it half made, and to allow it to become cold before it is finished. The other most common causes of failure are using yeast which is no longer sweet, or which has been frozen, or has had hot liquid poured over it.

As a general rule, the oven for baking bread should be rather quick and the heat so regulated as to penetrate the dough without hardening the outside. The oven door should not be opened after the bread is put in until the dough is set or has become firm, as the cool air admitted will have an unfavorable effect upon it.

The dough should rise and the bread begin to brown after about fifteen minutes, but only slightly. Bake from fifty to sixty minutes and have it brown, not black or whitey brown, but brown all over when well baked.

When the bread is baked, remove the loaves immediately from the pans and place them where the air will circulate freely around them, and thus carry off the gas which has been formed, but is no longer needed.

Never leave the bread in the pan or on a pin table to absorb the odor of the wood. If you like crusts that are crisp do not cover the loaves; but to give the soft, tender, wafer-like consistency which many prefer, wrap them while still hot in several thicknesses of bread-cloth. When cold put them in a stone jar, removing the cloth, as that absorbs the moisture and gives the bread an unpleasant taste and odor. Keep the jar well covered and carefully cleansed from crumbs and stale pieces. Scald and dry it thoroughly every two or three days. A yard and a half square of coarse table linen makes the best bread-cloth. Keep in good supply; use them for no other purpose.

Some people use scalding water in making wheat bread; in that case the flour must be scalded and allowed to cool before the yeast is added—then proceed as above. Bread made in this manner keeps moist in summer much longer than when made in the usual mode.

Home-made yeast is generally preferred to any other. Compressed yeast, as now sold in most grocery stores, makes fine light, sweet bread, and is a much quicker process, and can always be had fresh, being made fresh every day.

WHEAT BREAD.

Sift the flour into a large bread-pan or bowl; make a hole in the middle of it, and pour in the yeast in the ratio of half a teacupful of yeast to two quarts of flour; stir the yeast lightly, then pour in your "wetting," either milk or water, as you choose,—which use warm in winter and cold in summer; if you use water as "wetting," dissolve in it a bit of butter of the size of an egg,—if you use milk, no butter is necessary; stir in the "wetting" very lightly, but do not mix all the flour into it; then cover the pan with a thick blanket or towel, and set it, in winter, in a warm place to rise,—this is called "*putting the bread in sponge*." In summer the bread should not be wet over night. In the morning add a teaspoonful of salt and mix all the flour in the pan with the sponge, kneading it well; then let it stand two hours or more until it has risen quite light; then remove the dough to the molding-board and mold it for a long time, cutting it in pieces and molding them together again and again, until the dough is elastic under the pressure of your hand, using as little flour as possible; then make it into loaves, put the loaves into baking-tins. The loaves should come half way up the pan, and they should be allowed to rise until the bulk is doubled. When the loaves are ready to put into the oven, the oven should be ready to receive them. It should be hot enough to brown a teaspoonful of flour in five minutes. The heat should be greater at the bottom than at the top of the oven, and the fire so arranged as to give sufficient strength of heat through the baking without being replenished. Let them stand ten or fifteen minutes, prick them three or four times with a fork, bake in a quick oven from forty-five to sixty minutes.

If these directions are followed, you will obtain sweet, tender and wholesome bread. If by any mistake the dough becomes sour before you are ready to bake it, you can rectify it by adding a little dry super-carbonate of soda, molding the dough a long time to distribute the soda equally throughout the mass. All bread is better, if naturally sweet, without the soda; but *sour bread* you should never eat, if you desire good health.

Keep well covered in a tin box or large stone crock, which should be wiped out every day or two, and scalded and dried thoroughly in the sun once a week.

COMPRESSED YEAST BREAD.

Use for two loaves of bread three quarts of sifted flour, nearly a quart of warm water, a level tablespoonful of salt and an ounce of compressed yeast. Dissolve the yeast in a pint of lukewarm water; then stir into it enough flour to make a thick batter. Cover the bowl containing the batter or sponge with a thick folded cloth and set it in a warm place to rise; if the temperature of heat is properly attended to the sponge will be foamy and light in half an hour. Now stir into this sponge the salt dissolved in a little warm water, add the rest of the flour and sufficient warm water to make the dough stiff enough to knead; then knead it from five to ten minutes, divide it into loaves, knead again each loaf and put them into buttered baking tins; cover them with a double thick cloth and set again in a warm place to rise twice their height, then bake the same as any bread. This bread has the advantage of that made of home-made yeast as it is made inside of three hours, whereas the other requires from twelve to fourteen hours.

HOME-MADE YEAST.

Boil six large potatoes in three pints of water. Tie a handful of hops in a small muslin bag and boil with the potatoes; when thoroughly cooked drain the water on enough flour to make a thin batter; set this on the stove or range and scald it enough to cook the flour (this makes the yeast keep longer); remove it from the fire and when cool enough, add the potatoes mashed, also half a cup of sugar, half a tablespoonful of ginger, two of salt and a teacupful of yeast. Let it stand in a warm place, until it has thoroughly risen, then put it in a large mouthed jug and cork tightly; set away in a cool place. The jug should be scalded before putting in the yeast.

Two-thirds of a coffeecupful of this yeast will make four loaves.

UNRIVALED YEAST.

On one morning boil two ounces of the best hops in four quarts of water half an hour; strain it, and let the liquor cool to the consistency of new milk; then put it in an earthen bowl and add half a cupful of salt and half a cupful of brown sugar; beat up one quart of flour with some of the liquor; then mix all well together, and let it stand till the third day after; then add six medium-sized potatoes, boiled and mashed through a colander; let it stand a day, then strain and bottle and it is fit for use. It must be stirred frequently while it is making, and kept near a fire. One advantage of this yeast is its spontaneous fermentation, requiring the help of no old yeast; if care be taken to let it ferment well in the bowl, it may immediately be corked tightly. Be careful to keep it in a cool place. Before using it shake the bottle up well. It will keep in a cool place two months, and is best the latter part of the time. Use about the same quantity as of other yeast.

DRIED YEAST OR YEAST CAKES.

Make a pan of yeast the same as "Home-Made Yeast;" mix in with it corn meal that has been sifted and dried, kneading it well until it is thick enough to roll out, when it can be cut into cakes or crumble up. Spread out and dry thoroughly in the shade; keep in a dry place.

When it is convenient to get compressed yeast, it is much better and cheaper than to make your own, a saving of time and trouble. Almost all groceries keep it, delivered to them fresh made daily.

SALT-RAISING BREAD.

While getting breakfast in the morning, as soon as the tea-kettle has boiled, take a quart tin cup or an earthen quart milk pitcher, scald it, then fill one-third full of water about as warm as the finger could be held in; then to this add a teaspoonful of salt, a pinch of brown sugar and coarse flour enough to make a batter of about the right consistency for griddle-cakes. Set the cup, with the spoon in it, in a closed vessel half-filled with water moderately hot, but not scalding. Keep the temperature as nearly even as possible and add a teaspoonful of flour once or twice during the process of fermentation. The yeast ought to reach to the top of the bowl in about five hours. Sift your flour into a pan, make an opening in the centre and pour in your yeast. Have ready a pitcher of warm milk, salted, or milk and water (not too hot, or you will scald the yeast germs), and stir rapidly into a pulpy mass with a spoon. Cover this sponge closely and keep warm for an hour, then knead into loaves, adding flour to make the proper consistency. Place in warm, well-greased pans, cover closely and leave till it is light. Bake in a steady oven, and when done let all the hot steam escape. Wrap closely in damp towels and keep in closed earthen jars until it is wanted.

This, in our grandmothers' time, used to be considered the prize bread, on account of its being sweet and wholesome and required no prepared yeast to make it. Nowadays yeast-bread is made with very little trouble, as the yeast can be procured at almost any grocery.

BREAD FROM MILK YEAST.

At noon the day before baking, take half a cup of corn meal and pour over it enough sweet milk boiling hot to make it the thickness of batter-cakes. In the winter place it where it will keep warm. The next morning before breakfast pour into a pitcher a pint of boiling water; add one teaspoonful of soda and one of salt. When cool enough so that it will not scald the flour, add enough to make a stiff batter; then add the cup of meal set the day before. This will be full of little bubbles. Then place the pitcher in a kettle of warm water, cover the top with a folded towel and put it where it will keep warm, and you will be surprised to find how soon the yeast will be at the top of the pitcher. Then pour the yeast into a bread-pan; add a pint and a half of warm water, or half water and half milk, and flour enough to knead into loaves. Knead but little harder than for biscuit and bake as soon as it rises to the top of the tin. This recipe makes five large loaves. Do not allow it to get too light before baking, for it will make the bread dry and crumbling. A cup of this milk yeast is excellent to raise buckwheat cakes.

GRAHAM BREAD.

One teacupful of wheat flour, one-half teacupful of Porto Rico molasses, one-half cupful of good yeast, one teaspoonful of salt, one pint of warm water; add sufficient Graham flour to make the dough as stiff as can be stirred with a strong spoon; this is to be mixed at night; in the morning, add one teaspoonful of soda, dissolved in a little water; mix well, and pour into two medium-sized pans; they will be about half full; let it stand in a warm place until it rises to the top of the pans, then bake one hour in a pretty hot oven.

This should be covered about twenty minutes when first put into the oven with a thick brown paper, or an old tin cover; it prevents the upper crust hardening before the loaf is well-risen. If these directions are correctly followed the bread will not be heavy or sodden, as it has been tried for years and never failed.

GRAHAM BREAD. (Unfermented.)

Stir together three heaping teaspoonfuls of baking powder, three cups of Graham flour and one cup of white flour; then add a large teaspoonful of salt and half a cup of sugar. Mix all thoroughly with milk or water into as stiff a batter as can be stirred with a spoon. If water is used, a lump of butter as large as a walnut may be melted and stirred into it. Bake immediately in well-greased pans.

BOSTON BROWN BREAD.

One pint of rye flour, one quart of corn meal, one teacupful of Graham flour, all fresh; half a teacupful of molasses or brown sugar, a teaspoonful of salt, and two-thirds of a teacupful of home-made yeast. Mix into as stiff a dough as can be stirred with a spoon, using warm water for wetting. Let it rise several hours, or over night; in the morning, or when light, add a teaspoonful of soda dissolved in a spoonful of warm water; beat it well and turn it into well-greased, deep bread-pans, and let it rise again. Bake in a *moderate* oven from three to four hours.

Palmer House, Chicago.

BOSTON BROWN BREAD. (Unfermented.)

One cupful of rye flour, two cupfuls of corn meal, one cupful of white flour, half a teacupful of molasses or sugar, a teaspoonful of salt. Stir all together *thoroughly*, and wet up with sour milk; then add a level teaspoonful of soda dissolved in a tablespoonful of water. The same can be made of sweet milk by substituting baking powder for soda. The batter to be stirred as thick as can be with a spoon, and turned into well-greased pans.

VIRGINIA BROWN BREAD.

One pint of corn meal; pour over enough boiling water to thoroughly scald it; when cool add one pint of light, white bread sponge, mix well together, add one cupful of molasses, and Graham flour enough to mold; this will make two loaves; when light, bake in a moderate oven one and a half hours.

RHODE ISLAND BROWN BREAD.

Two and one-half cupfuls of corn meal, one and one-half cupfuls of rye meal, one egg, one cup of molasses, two teaspoonfuls of cream of tartar, one teaspoonful of soda, a little salt and one quart of milk. Bake in a covered dish, either earthen or iron, in a moderately hot oven three hours.

STEAMED BROWN BREAD.

One cup of white flour, two of Graham flour, two of Indian meal, one teaspoonful of soda, one cup of molasses, three and a half cups of milk, a little salt. Beat well and steam for four hours. This is for sour milk; when sweet milk is used, use baking powder in place of soda.

This is improved by setting it into the oven fifteen minutes after it is slipped from the mold. To be eaten warm with butter. Most excellent.

RYE BREAD.

To a quart of warm water stir as much wheat flour as will make a smooth batter; stir into it half a gill of home-made yeast, and set it in a warm place to rise; this is called setting a sponge; let it be mixed in some vessel which will contain twice the quantity; in the morning, put three pounds and a half of rye flour into a bowl or tray, make a hollow in the centre, pour in the sponge, add a dessertspoonful of salt, and half a small teaspoonful of soda, dissolved in a little water; make the whole into a smooth dough, with as much warm water as may be necessary; knead it well, cover it, and let it set in a warm place for three hours; then knead it again, and make it into two or three loaves; bake in a quick oven one hour, if made in two loaves, or less if the loaves are smaller.

RYE AND CORN BREAD.

One quart of rye meal or rye flour, two quarts of Indian meal, scalded (by placing in a pan and pouring over it just enough *boiling* water to merely wet it, but not enough to make it into a batter, stirring constantly with a spoon), one-half cup of molasses, two teaspoonfuls salt, one teacup yeast, make it as stiff as can be stirred with a spoon, mixing with warm water and let rise all night. In the morning add a level teaspoonful of soda dissolved in a little water; then put it in a large pan, smooth the top with the hand dipped in cold water; let it stand a short time and bake five or six hours. If put in the oven late in the day, let it remain all night.

Graham may be used instead of rye, and baked as above.

This is similar to the "Rye and Injun" of our grandmothers' days, but that was placed in a kettle, allowed to rise, then placed in a covered iron pan upon the hearth before the fire, with coals heaped upon the lid, to bake all night.

FRENCH BREAD.

Beat together one pint of milk, four tablespoonfuls of melted butter, or half butter and half lard, half a cupful of yeast, one teaspoonful of salt and two eggs. Stir into this two quarts of flour. When this dough is risen, make into two large rolls and bake as any bread. Cut across the top diagonal gashes just before putting into the oven.

TWIST BREAD.

Let the bread be made as directed for wheat bread, then take three pieces as large as a pint bowl each; strew a little flour over the paste-board or table, roll each piece under your hands to twelve inches length, making it smaller in circumference at the ends than in the middle; having rolled the three in this way, take a baking-tin, lay one part on it, joint one end of each of the other two to it, and braid them together the length of the rolls and join the ends by pressing them together; dip a brush in milk and pass it over the top of the loaf; after ten minutes or so, set it in a quick oven and bake for nearly an hour.

NEW ENGLAND CORN CAKE.

One quart of milk, one pint of corn meal, one teacupful of wheat flour, a teaspoonful of salt, two tablespoonfuls of melted butter. Scald the milk and gradually pour it on the meal; when cool add the butter and salt, also a half cup of yeast. Do this at night; in the morning beat thoroughly and add two well-beaten eggs, and a half teaspoonful of soda, dissolved in a spoonful of water. Pour the mixture into buttered deep earthen plates, let it stand fifteen minutes to rise again, then bake from twenty to thirty minutes.

GERMAN BREAD.

One pint of milk well boiled, one teacupful of sugar, two tablespoonfuls of nice lard or butter, two-thirds of a teacupful of baker's yeast. Make a rising with the milk and yeast; when light, mix in the sugar and shortening, with flour enough to make as soft a dough as can be handled. Flour the paste-board well, roll out about one-half inch thick; put this quantity into two large pans; make about a dozen indentures with the finger on the top; put a small piece of butter in each, and sift over the whole one tablespoonful of sugar mixed with one teaspoonful of cinnamon. Let this stand for a second rising; when perfectly light, bake in a quick oven fifteen or twenty minutes.

CORN BREAD.

Two cups of sifted meal, half a cup of flour, two cups of sour milk, two well-beaten eggs, half a cup of molasses or sugar, a teaspoonful of salt, two tablespoonfuls of melted butter. Mix the meal and flour smoothly and gradually with the milk, then the butter, molasses and salt, then the beaten eggs, and lastly dissolve a level teaspoonful of baking soda in a little milk and beat thoroughly altogether. Bake nearly an hour in well-buttered tins, not very shallow. This recipe can be made with sweet milk by using baking powder in place of soda.

St. Charles Hotel, New Orleans.

VIRGINIA CORN BREAD.

Three cups of white corn meal, one cup of flour, one tablespoonful of sugar, one teaspoonful of salt, two heaping teaspoonfuls of baking powder, one tablespoonful of lard, three cups of milk and three eggs. Sift together the flour, corn meal, sugar, salt and baking powder; rub in the lard cold, add the eggs well beaten and then the milk. Mix into a moderately stiff batter; pour it into well-greased, shallow baking pans (pie-tins are suitable). Bake from thirty to forty minutes.

BOSTON CORN BREAD.

One cup of sweet milk, two of sour milk, two-thirds of a cup of molasses, one of wheat flour, four of corn meal and one teaspoonful of soda; steam for three hours, and brown a few minutes in the oven. The same made of sweet milk and baking powder is equally as good.

INDIAN LOAF CAKE.

Mix a teacupful of powdered white sugar with a quart of rich milk, and cut up in the milk two ounces of butter, adding a saltspoonful of salt. Put this mixture into a covered pan or skillet, and set it on the fire till it is scalding hot. Then take it off, and scald with it as much yellow Indian meal (previously sifted) as will make it of the consistency of thick boiled mush. Beat the whole very hard for a quarter of an hour, and then set it away to cool.

While it is cooling, beat three eggs very light, and stir them gradually into the mixture when it is about as warm as new milk. Add a teacupful of good strong yeast and beat the whole another quarter of an hour, for much of the goodness of this cake depends on its being long and well beaten. Then have ready a tin mold or earthen pan with a pipe in the centre (to diffuse the heat through the middle of the cake). The pan must be very well-buttered as Indian meal is apt to stick. Put in the mixture, cover it and set it in a warm place to rise. It should be light in about four hours. Then bake it two hours in a moderate oven. When done, turn it out with the broad surface downwards and send it to table hot and whole. Cut it into slices and eat it with butter.

This will be found an excellent cake. If wanted for breakfast, mix it and set it to rise the night before. If properly made, standing all night will not injure it. Like all Indian cakes (of which this is one of the best), it should be eaten warm.

St. Charles Hotel, New Orleans.

JOHNNIE CAKE.

Sift one quart of Indian meal into a pan; make a hole in the middle and pour in a pint of warm water, adding one teaspoonful of salt; with a spoon mix the meal and water gradually into a soft dough; stir it very briskly for a quarter of an hour or more, till it becomes light and spongy; then spread the dough smoothly and evenly on a straight, flat board (a piece of the head of a flour-barrel will serve for this purpose); place the board nearly upright before an open fire and put an iron against the back to support it; bake it well; when done, cut it in squares; send it hot to table, split and buttered.

Old Plantation Style.

SPIDER CORN-CAKE.

Beat two eggs and one-fourth cup sugar together. Then add one cup sweet milk and one cup of sour milk in which you have dissolved one teaspoonful soda. Add a teaspoonful of salt. Then mix one and two-thirds cups of granulated corn meal and one-third cup flour with this. Put a spider or skillet on the range and when it is hot melt in two tablespoonfuls of butter. Turn the spider so that the butter can run up on the sides of the pan. Pour in the corn-cake mixture and add one more cup of sweet milk, but do not stir afterwards. Put this in the oven and bake from twenty to thirty-five minutes. When done, there should be a streak of custard through it.

SOUTHERN CORN MEAL PONE OR CORN DODGERS.

Mix with cold water into a soft dough one quart of southern corn meal, sifted, a teaspoonful of salt, a tablespoonful of butter or lard melted. Mold into oval cakes with the hands and bake in a very hot oven, in well-greased pans. To be eaten hot. The crust should be brown.

RAISED POTATO-CAKE.

Potato-cakes, to be served with roast lamb or with game, are made of equal quantities of mashed potatoes and of flour, say one quart of each, two tablespoonfuls of butter, a little salt and milk enough to make a batter as for griddle-cakes; to this allow half a teacupful of fresh yeast; let it rise till it is light and bubbles of air form; then dissolve half a teaspoonful of soda in a spoonful of warm water and add to the batter; bake in muffin tins. These are good also with fricasseed chicken; take them from the tins and drop in the gravy just before sending to the table.

BISCUITS, ROLLS, MUFFINS, ETC.

GENERAL SUGGESTIONS.

In making batter-cakes, the ingredients should be put together over night to rise, and the eggs and butter added in the morning; the butter melted and eggs well beaten. If the batter appears sour in the least, dissolve a little soda and stir into it; this should be done early enough to rise some time before baking.

Water can be used in place of milk in all raised dough, and the dough should be thoroughly light before making into loaves or biscuits; then when molding them use as little flour as possible; the kneading to be done when first made from the sponge, and should be done well and for some length of time, as this makes the pores fine, the bread cut smooth and tender. Care should be taken not to get the dough too stiff.

Where any recipe calls for baking powder, and you do not have it, you can use cream of tartar and soda, in the proportion of one level teaspoonful of soda to two of cream of tartar.

When the recipe calls for sweet milk or cream, and you do not have it, you may use in place of it sour milk or cream, and, in that case, baking powder or cream of tartar *must not* be used, but baking-soda, using a *level* teaspoonful to a quart of sour milk; the milk is always best when just turned, so that it is solid, and not sour enough to whey or to be watery.

When making biscuits or bread with baking powder or soda and cream of tartar, the oven should be prepared first; the dough handled quickly and put into the oven immediately, as soon as it becomes the proper lightness, to ensure good success. If the oven is *too slow*, the article baked will be heavy and hard.

As in beating cake, never *stir* ingredients into batter, but beat them in, by beating down from the bottom, and up, and over again. This laps the air into the batter which produces little air-cells and causes the dough to puff and swell as it comes in contact with the heat while cooking.

TO RENEW STALE ROLLS.

To freshen stale biscuits or rolls, put them into a steamer for ten minutes, then dry them off in a hot oven; or dip each roll for an instant in cold water and heat them crisp in the oven.

WARM BREAD FOR BREAKFAST..

Dough after it has become once sufficiently raised and perfectly light, cannot afterwards be injured by setting aside in any cold place where it cannot *freeze*; therefore, biscuits, rolls, etc., can be made late the day before wanted for breakfast. Prepare them ready for baking by molding them out late in the evening; lay them a little apart on buttered tins; cover the tins with a cloth, then fold around that a newspaper, so as to exclude the air, as that has a tendency to cause the crust to be hard and thick when baked. The best place in summer is to place them in the ice-box, then all you have to do in the morning (an hour before breakfast time, and while the oven is heating) is to bring them from the ice-box, take off the cloth and warm it, and place it over them again; then set the tins in a warm place near the fire. This will give them time to rise and bake when needed. If these directions are followed rightly, you will find it makes no difference with their lightness and goodness, and you can always be sure of warm raised biscuits for breakfast in one hour's time.

Stale rolls may be made light and flakey by dipping for a moment in cold water, and placing immediately in a very hot oven to be made crisp and hot.

SODA BISCUIT.

One quart of sifted flour, one teaspoonful of soda, two teaspoonfuls of cream of tartar, one teaspoonful of salt; mix thoroughly, and rub in two tablespoonfuls of butter and wet with one pint of sweet milk. Bake in a quick oven.

BAKING POWDER BISCUIT.

Two pints of flour, butter the size of an egg, three heaping teaspoonfuls of baking powder and one teaspoonful of salt; make a soft dough of sweet milk or water, knead as little as possible, cut out with the usual biscuit-cutter and bake in rather a quick oven.

SOUR MILK BISCUIT.

Rub into a quart of sifted flour a piece of butter the size of an egg, one teaspoonful of salt; stir into this a pint of sour milk, dissolve one teaspoonful of soda and stir into the milk just as you add it to the flour; knead it up quickly, roll it out nearly half an inch thick and cut out with a biscuit-cutter; bake immediately in a quick oven.

Very nice biscuit may be made with sour cream without the butter by the same process.

RAISED BISCUIT.

Sift two quarts of flour in a mixing-pan, make a hole in the middle of the flour, pour into this one pint of warm water or new milk, one teaspoonful of salt, half a cup of melted lard or butter, stir in a little flour, then add half a cupful of yeast, after which stir in as much flour as you can conveniently with your hand, let it rise over night; in the morning add nearly a teaspoonful of soda, and more flour as is needed to make a rather soft dough; then mold fifteen to twenty minutes, the longer the better; let it rise until light again, roll this out about half an inch thick and cut out with a biscuit-cutter, or make it into little balls with your hands; cover and set in a warm place to rise. When light, bake a light brown in a moderate oven. Rub a little warm butter or sweet lard on the sides of the biscuits when you place them on the tins, to prevent their sticking together when baked.

LIGHT BISCUIT. No. 1.

Take a piece of bread dough that will make about as many biscuits as you wish; lay it out rather flat in a bowl; break into it two eggs, half a cup of sugar, half a cup of butter; mix this thoroughly with enough flour to keep it from sticking to the hands and board. Knead it well for about fifteen or twenty minutes, make into small biscuits, place in a greased pan, and let them rise until about even with the top of the pan. Bake in a quick oven for about half an hour.

These can be made in the form of rolls, which some prefer.

LIGHT BISCUIT. No. 2.

When you bake take a pint of sponge, one tablespoonful of melted butter, one tablespoonful of sugar, the white of one egg beaten to a foam. Let rise until light, mold into biscuits, and when light bake.

GRAHAM BISCUITS, WITH YEAST.

Take one pint of water or milk, one large tablespoonful of butter, two tablespoonfuls of sugar, a half cup of yeast and a pinch of salt; take enough wheat flour to use up the water, making it the consistency of batter-cakes; add the rest of the ingredients and as much Graham flour as can be stirred in with a spoon; set it away till morning; in the morning grease a pan, flour your hands, take a lump of dough the size of an egg, roll it lightly between the palms of your hands, let them rise twenty minutes, and bake in a tolerably hot oven.

EGG BISCUIT.

Sift together a quart of dry flour and three heaping teaspoonfuls of baking powder. Rub into this thoroughly a piece of butter the size of an egg; add two well-beaten eggs, a tablespoonful of sugar, a teaspoonful of salt. Mix all together quickly into a soft dough, with one cup of milk, or more if needed. Roll out nearly half of an inch thick. Cut into biscuits, and bake immediately in a quick oven from fifteen to twenty minutes.

PARKER HOUSE ROLLS.

One pint of milk, boiled and cooled, a piece of butter the size of an egg, one-half cupful of fresh yeast, one tablespoonful of sugar, one pinch of salt, and two quarts of sifted flour.

Melt the butter in the warm milk, then add the sugar, salt and flour, and let it rise over night. Mix rather soft. In the morning, add to this half of a teaspoonful of soda dissolved in a spoonful of water. Mix in enough flour to make the same stiffness as any biscuit dough; roll out not more than a quarter of an inch thick. Cut with a large round cutter; spread soft butter over the tops and fold one-half over the other by doubling it. Place them apart a little so that there will be room to rise. Cover and place them near the fire for fifteen or twenty minutes before baking. Bake in rather a quick oven.

PARKER HOUSE ROLLS. (Unfermented.)

These rolls are made with baking powder, and are much sooner made, although the preceding recipe is the old original one from the "Parker House." Stir into a quart of sifted flour three large teaspoonfuls of baking powder, a tablespoonful of cold butter, a teaspoonful of salt and one of sugar, and a well-beaten egg; rub all well into the flour, pour in a pint of cold milk, mix up quickly into a smooth dough, roll it out less than half an inch thick, cut with a large biscuit-cutter, spread soft butter over the top of each; fold one-half over the other by doubling it, lay them a little apart on greased tins. Set them immediately in a pretty hot oven. Rub over the tops with sweet milk before putting in the oven, to give them a glaze.

FRENCH ROLLS.

Three cups of sweet milk, one cup of butter and lard, mixed in equal proportions, one-half cup of good yeast, or half a cake of compressed yeast, and a teaspoonful of salt. Add flour enough to make a stiff dough. Let it rise over night; in the morning, add two well-beaten eggs; knead thoroughly and let it rise again. With the hands, make it into balls as large as an egg; then roll between the hands to make *long rolls* (about three inches). Place close together in even rows on well-buttered pans. Cover and let them rise again, then bake in a quick oven to a delicate brown.

BEATEN BISCUIT.

Two quarts of sifted flour, a teaspoonful of salt, a tablespoonful of sweet lard, one egg; make up with half a pint of milk, or if milk is not to be had, plain water will answer; beat well until the dough blisters and cracks; pull off a two-inch square of the dough; roll it into a ball with the hand; flatten, stick with a fork, and bake in a quick oven.

It is not beating hard that makes the biscuit nice, but the regularity of the motion. Beating hard, the old cooks say, *kills* the dough.

An old-fashioned Southern Recipe.

POTATO BISCUIT.

Boil six good-sized potatoes with their jackets on; take them out with a skimmer, drain and squeeze with a towel to ensure being dry; then remove the skin, mash them perfectly free from lumps, add a tablespoonful of butter, one egg and a pint of sweet milk. When cool, beat in half a cup of yeast. Put in just enough flour to make a stiff dough. When this rises, make into small cakes. Let them rise the same as biscuit and bake a delicate brown.

This dough is very fine dropped into meat soups for pot-pie.

VINEGAR BISCUITS.

Take two quarts of flour, one large tablespoonful of lard or butter, one tablespoonful and a half of vinegar and one teaspoonful of soda; put the soda in the vinegar and stir it well; stir in the flour; beat two eggs very light and add to it; make a dough with warm water stiff enough to roll out, and cut with a biscuit-cutter one inch thick and bake in a *quick* oven.

GRAFTON MILK BISCUITS.

Boil and mash two white potatoes; add two teaspoonfuls of brown sugar; pour boiling water over these, enough to soften them. When tepid, add one small teacupful of yeast; when light, warm three ounces of butter in one pint of milk, a little salt, a third of a teaspoonful of soda and flour enough to make stiff sponge; when risen, work it on the board, put it back in the tray to rise again; when risen, roll into cakes and let them stand half an hour. Bake in a *quick* oven. These biscuits are fine.

SALLY LUNN.

Warm one-half cupful of butter in a pint of milk; add a teaspoonful of salt, a tablespoonful of sugar, and seven cupfuls of *sifted* flour; beat thoroughly and when the mixture is blood warm, add four beaten eggs and last of all, half a cup of good lively yeast. Beat hard until the batter breaks in blisters. Set it to rise over night. In the morning, dissolve half a teaspoonful of soda, stir it into the batter and turn it into a well-buttered, shallow dish to rise again about fifteen or twenty minutes. Bake about fifteen to twenty minutes.

The cake should be torn apart, not cut; cutting with a knife makes warm bread heavy. Bake a light brown. This cake is frequently seen on Southern tables.

SALLY LUNN. (Unfermented.)

Rub a piece of butter as large as an egg into a quart of flour; add a tumbler of milk, two eggs, three tablespoonfuls of sugar, three tablespoonfuls of baking powder and a teaspoonful of salt. Scatter the baking powder, salt and sugar into the flour; add the eggs, the butter, melted, the milk. Stir all together and bake in well-greased round pans. Eat warm with butter.

LONDON HOT-CROSS BUNS.

Three cups of milk, one cup of yeast, or one cake of compressed yeast dissolved in a cup of tepid water, and flour enough to make a thick batter; set this as a sponge over night. In the morning add half a cup of melted butter, one cup of sugar, half a nutmeg grated, one saltspoonful of salt, half a teaspoonful of soda, and flour enough to roll out like biscuit. Knead well and set to rise for five hours. Roll the dough half an inch thick; cut in round cakes and lay in rows in a buttered baking-pan, and let the cakes stand half an hour, or until light; then put them in the oven, having first made a deep cross on each with a knife. Bake a light brown and brush over with white of egg beaten stiff with powdered sugar.

RUSKS, WITH YEAST.

In one large coffeecup of warm milk dissolve half a cake of compressed yeast, or three tablespoonfuls of home-made yeast; to this add three well-beaten eggs, a small cup of sugar and a teaspoonful of salt; beat these together. Use flour enough to make a smooth, light dough, let it stand until very light, then knead it in the form of biscuits; place them on buttered tins and let them rise until they are almost up to the edge of the tins; pierce the top of each one and bake in a quick oven. Glaze the top of each with sugar and milk, or the white of an egg, before baking. Some add dried currants, well-washed and dried in the oven.

RUSKS.

Two cups of raised dough, one of sugar, half a cup of butter, two well-beaten eggs, flour enough to make a stiff dough; set to rise, and when light mold into high biscuit and let rise again; rub damp sugar and cinnamon over the top and place in the oven. Bake about twenty minutes.

RUSKS. (Unfermented.)

Three cups of flour sifted, three teaspoonfuls of baking powder, one teaspoonful of salt, three tablespoonfuls of sugar, two tablespoonfuls of butter, three eggs, half a nutmeg grated and a teaspoonful of ground cinnamon, two small cups of milk; sift together salt, flour, sugar and baking powder; rub in the butter cold; add the milk, beaten eggs and spices; mix into a soft dough, break off pieces about as large as an egg, roll them under the hands into round balls, rub the tops with sugar and water mixed, and then sprinkle dry sugar over them. Bake immediately.

SCOTCH SCONES.

Thoroughly mix, while dry, one quart of sifted flour, loosely measured, with two heaping teaspoonfuls of baking powder; then rub into it a tablespoonful of cold butter and a teaspoonful of salt. Be sure that the butter is well worked in. Add sweet milk enough to make a *very* soft paste. Roll out the paste about a quarter of an inch thick, using plenty of flour on the paste-board and rolling pin. Cut it into triangular pieces, each side about four inches long. Flour the sides and bottom of a biscuit tin, and place the pieces on it. Bake immediately in a quick oven from twenty to thirty minutes. When half done, brush over with sweet milk. Some cooks prefer to bake them on a floured griddle, and cut them a round shape the size of a saucer, then scarred across to form four quarters.

CRACKNELS.

Two cups of rich milk, four tablespoonfuls of butter and a gill of yeast, a teaspoonful of salt; mix warm, add flour enough to make a light dough.

When light, roll thin and cut in long pieces three inches wide, prick well with a fork and bake in a slow oven. They are to be mixed rather hard and rolled very thin, like soda crackers.

RAISED MUFFINS. No. 1.

Make a batter of one pint of sweet milk, one teaspoonful of sugar, one of salt, a tablespoonful of butter or sweet lard and a half cup of yeast; add flour enough to make it moderately thick; keep it in a warm, *not hot*, place until it is quite light, then stir in one or two well-beaten eggs, and half a teaspoonful of soda, dissolved in a little warm water. Let the batter stand twenty-five or thirty minutes longer to rise a little, turn into well-greased muffin-rings or gem-pans, and bake in a quick oven.

To be served hot and torn open, instead of cut with a knife.

RAISED MUFFINS. No. 2.

Three pints of flour, three eggs, a piece of butter the size of an egg, two heaping teaspoonfuls of white sugar, one-half cake of compressed yeast and a quart of milk; warm the milk with the butter in it; cool a little, stir in the sugar and add a little salt; stir this gradually into the flour, then add the eggs well beaten; dissolve the yeast in half a cup of lukewarm water and add to the other ingredients; if the muffins are wanted for luncheon, mix them about eight o'clock in the morning; if for breakfast, set them at ten o'clock at night; when ready for baking, stir in half a teaspoonful of soda dissolved in a teaspoonful of hot water; butter the muffin-rings or gem-irons and bake in a quick oven.

EGG MUFFINS. (Fine.)

One quart of flour, sifted twice; three eggs, the whites and yolks beaten separately, three teacups of sweet milk, a teaspoonful of salt, a tablespoonful of sugar, a large tablespoonful of lard or butter and two heaping teaspoonfuls of baking powder. Sift together flour, sugar, salt and baking powder; rub in the lard cold, add the beaten eggs and milk; mix quickly into a smooth batter, a little firmer than for griddle-cakes. Grease well some muffin-pans and fill them two-thirds full. Bake in a hot oven fifteen or twenty minutes. These made of cream, omitting the butter, are excellent.

PLAIN MUFFINS.

One egg well beaten, a tablespoonful of butter and a tablespoonful of sugar, with a teaspoonful of salt, all beaten until very light. One cup of milk, three of sifted flour and three teaspoonfuls of baking powder. One-half Graham and one-half rye meal may be used instead of wheat flour, or two cups of corn meal and one of flour.

Drop on well-greased patty-pans and bake twenty minutes in a rather quick oven, or bake on a griddle in muffin-rings.

MUFFINS WITHOUT EGGS.

One quart of buttermilk, a teaspoonful of soda dissolved in the milk, a little salt, and flour enough to make a stiff batter. Drop in hot gem-pans and bake in a quick oven. Two or three tablespoonfuls of sour cream will make them a little richer.

TENNESSEE MUFFINS.

One pint of corn meal, one pint of flour, one tablespoonful of sugar, one teaspoonful of salt, three of baking powder, one tablespoonful of lard or butter, two eggs and a pint of milk. Sift together corn meal, flour, sugar, salt and powder; rub in lard or butter cold, and eggs beaten and milk; mix into batter of consistency of cup-cake; muffin-rings to be cold and well greased, then fill two-thirds full. Bake in hot oven fifteen minutes.

CORN MEAL MUFFINS. (Without Eggs.)

One cup of flour, one cup of corn meal, two tablespoonfuls of sugar, water to make a thick batter, or sour milk is better; mix at night; in the morning add two tablespoonfuls of melted butter and one teaspoonful of soda; bake in cake rounds.

HOMINY MUFFINS.

Two cups of boiled hominy; beat it smooth, stir in three cups of sour milk, half a cup of melted butter, two teaspoonfuls of salt, two tablespoonfuls of sugar; add three eggs well beaten, one teaspoonful of soda dissolved in hot water, two cups of flour. Bake quickly.

Rice muffins may be made in the same manner.

GRAHAM GEMS. No. 1.

Two cupfuls of Graham flour, one cupful of wheat flour, two teaspoonfuls of baking powder, a tablespoonful of sugar, one of salt and one well-beaten egg.

Mix with sweet milk to make a thin batter; beat it well. Bake in gem-irons; have the irons well greased; fill two-thirds full and bake in a hot oven. Will bake in from fifteen to twenty minutes.

GRAHAM GEMS. No. 2.

Three cups of sour milk, one teaspoonful of soda, one of salt, one tablespoonful of brown sugar, one of melted lard or butter, one or two beaten eggs; to the egg add the milk, then the sugar and salt, then the Graham flour (with the soda mixed in), together with the lard or butter; make a stiff batter, so that it will *drop,* not pour, from the spoon. Have the gem-pans very hot, fill and bake fifteen minutes in a hot oven.

The same can be made of sweet milk, using three teaspoonfuls of baking powder instead of soda, and if you use sweet milk, put in no shortening. Excellent.

Muffins of all kinds should only be cut just around the edge, then pulled open with the fingers.

PLAIN GRAHAM GEMS.

Two cupfuls of the best Graham meal, two of water, fresh and cold, or milk and water, and a little salt. Stir briskly for a minute or two. Have the gem-pan, hot and well greased, on the top of the stove while pouring in the batter. Then place in a very hot oven and bake forty minutes. It is best to check the heat a little when they are nearly done. As the best prepared gems may be spoiled if the heat is not sufficient, care and judgment must be used in order to secure this most healthful as well, as delicious bread.

WAFFLES.

Take a quart of flour and wet it with a little sweet milk that has been boiled and cooled, then stir in enough of the milk to form a thick batter. Add a tablespoonful of melted butter, a teaspoonful of salt, and yeast to raise it. When light add two well-beaten eggs, heat your waffle-iron, grease it well and fill it with the batter. Two or three minutes will suffice to bake on one side; then turn the iron over, and when brown on both sides the cake is done. Serve immediately.

CONTINENTAL HOTEL WAFFLES.

Put into one quart of sifted flour three teaspoonfuls of baking powder, one teaspoonful of salt, one of sugar, all thoroughly stirred and sifted together; add a tablespoonful of melted butter, six well-beaten eggs and a pint of sweet milk; cook in waffle-irons heated and well greased. Serve hot.

NEWPORT WAFFLES.

Make one pint of Indian meal into mush in the usual way. While hot, put in a small lump of butter and a dessertspoonful of salt. Set the mush aside to cool. Meanwhile, beat separately till very light the whites and yolks of four eggs. Add the eggs to the mush, and cream in gradually one quart of wheaten flour. Add half a pint of buttermilk, or sour cream, in which has been dissolved half a teaspoonful of carbonate of soda. Lastly, bring to the consistency of thin batter by the addition of sweet milk. Waffle-irons should be put on to heat an hour in advance, that they may be in the proper condition for baking as soon as the batter is ready. Have a brisk fire, butter the irons thoroughly, but with nicety, and bake quickly. Fill the irons only half full of batter, that the waffles may have room to rise.

CREAM WAFFLES.

One pint of sour cream, two eggs, one pint of flour, one tablespoonful of corn meal, one teaspoonful of soda, half a teaspoonful of salt. Beat the eggs separately, mix the cream with the beaten yolks, stir in the flour, corn meal and salt; add the soda dissolved in a little sweet milk, and, lastly, the whites beaten to a stiff froth.

RICE WAFFLES. No. 1.

One quart of flour, half a teaspoonful of salt, one teaspoonful of sugar, two teaspoonfuls of baking powder, one large tablespoonful of butter, two eggs, one and a half pints of milk, one cupful of hot boiled rice. Sift the flour, salt, sugar and baking powder well together; rub the butter into the flour; beat the eggs well, separately, and add the stiff whites last of all.

RICE WAFFLES. No. 2.

Rub through a sieve one pint of boiled rice, add it to a tablespoonful of dry flour, two-thirds of a teaspoonful of salt, two teaspoonfuls of baking powder. Beat separately the yolks and whites of three eggs; add to the yolks a cup and a half of milk, work it into the flour, then add an ounce of melted butter; beat the whites of eggs thoroughly; mix the whole together. Heat the waffle-iron and grease it evenly; pour the batter into the half of the iron over the range until nearly two-thirds full, cover, allow to cook a moment, then turn and brown slightly on the other side.

GERMAN RICE WAFFLES.

Boil a half pound of rice in milk until it becomes thoroughly soft Then remove it from the fire, stirring it constantly, and adding, a little at a time, one quart of sifted flour, five beaten eggs, two spoonfuls of yeast, a half pound of melted butter, a little salt and a teacupful of warm milk. Set the batter in a warm place, and, when risen, bake in the ordinary way.

BERRY TEA-CAKES.

Nice little tea-cakes to be baked in muffin-rings are made of one cup of sugar, two eggs, one and a half cups of milk, one heaping teaspoonful of baking powder, a piece of butter the size of an egg and flour sufficient to make a stiff batter. In this batter stir a pint bowl of fruit—any fresh are nice—or canned berries with the juice poured off. Serve while warm and they are a dainty addition to the tea-table. Eaten with butter.

RYE DROP-CAKES.

One pint of warm milk, with half a teaspoonful of soda dissolved in it, a little salt, four eggs well beaten, and rye flour enough to make a thin batter; bake in small cups, buttered, and in a hot oven, or in small cakes upon a hot griddle.

WHEAT DROP-CAKES.

One pint of cream, six eggs well beaten, a little salt, and wheat flour enough to make a thin batter; bake in little cups buttered and in a hot oven fifteen minutes.

POP-OVERS.

Two cups of flour, two cups of sweet milk, two eggs, one teaspoonful of butter, one teaspoonful of salt, bake in cups in a quick oven fifteen minutes. Serve hot with a sweet sauce.

FLANNEL CAKES. (With Yeast.)

Heat a pint of sweet milk and into it put two heaping tablespoonfuls of butter, let it melt, then add a pint of cold milk and the well-beaten yolks of four eggs—placing the whites in a cool place; also, a teaspoonful of salt, four tablespoonfuls of home-made yeast and sufficient flour to make a stiff batter; set it in a warm place to rise; let it stand three hours or over night; before baking add the beaten whites; bake like any other griddle-cakes. Be sure to make the batter stiff enough, for flour must not be added after it has risen, unless it is allowed to rise again. These, half corn meal and half wheat, are very nice.

FEATHER GRIDDLE-CAKES. (With Yeast.)

Make a batter, at night, of a pint of water or milk, a teaspoonful of salt, and half a teacupful of yeast; in the morning, add to it one teacupful of thick, sour milk, two eggs well beaten, a level tablespoonful of melted butter, a level teaspoonful of soda and flour enough to make the consistency of pancake batter; let stand twenty minutes, then bake.

This is a convenient way, when making sponge for bread over night, using some of the sponge.

WHEAT GRIDDLE-CAKES.

Three cups of flour, one teaspoonful of salt, three teaspoonfuls of baking powder sifted together; beat three eggs and add to three cupfuls of sweet milk, also a tablespoonful of melted butter; mix all into a smooth batter, as thick as will run in a stream from the lips of a pitcher. Bake on a well-greased, hot griddle, a nice light brown. Very good.

SOUR MILK GRIDDLE-CAKES.

Make a batter of a quart of sour milk and as much sifted flour as is needed to thicken so that it will run from the dish; add two beaten eggs, a teaspoonful of salt, a tablespoonful of melted butter, and a level teaspoonful of soda dissolved in a little milk or cold water, added last; then bake on a hot griddle, well greased, brown on both sides.

CORN MEAL GRIDDLE-CAKES. (With Yeast.)

Stir into one quart of boiling milk three cups of corn meal; after it cools add one cup of white flour, a teaspoonful of salt and three tablespoonfuls of home-made yeast. Mix this over night. In the morning add one tablespoonful of melted butter or lard, two beaten eggs and a teaspoonful of soda dissolved in a little water.

This batter should stand a few minutes, after adding the butter and soda, that it should have time to rise a little; in the meantime the griddle could be heating. Take a small stick like a good-sized skewer, wind a bit of cloth around the end of it, fasten it by winding a piece of thread around that and tying it firm. Melt together a tablespoonful of butter and lard. Grease the griddle with this. Between each batch of cakes, wipe the griddle off with a clean paper or cloth and grease afresh. Put the cakes on by spoonfuls, or pour them carefully from a pitcher, trying to get them as near the same size as possible. As soon as they begin to bubble all over turn them, and cook on the other side till they stop puffing. The second lot always cooks better than the first, as the griddle becomes evenly heated.

CORN MEAL GRIDDLE-CAKES.

Scald two cups of sifted meal, mix with a cup of wheat flour and a teaspoonful of salt. Add three well-beaten eggs; thin the whole with sour milk enough to make it the right consistency. Beat the whole till very light and add a teaspoonful of baking soda dissolved in a little water. If you use sweet milk, use two large teaspoonfuls of baking powder instead of soda.

GRIDDLE-CAKES. (Very Good.)

One quart of Graham flour, half a pint of Indian meal, one gill of yeast, a teaspoonful of salt; mix the flour and meal, pour on enough warm water to make batter rather thicker than that for buckwheat cakes, add the yeast, and when light bake on griddle not too hot.

GRAHAM GRIDDLE-CAKES.

Mix together dry two cups of Graham flour, one cup wheat flour, two heaping teaspoonfuls of baking powder and one teaspoonful of salt. Then add three eggs well beaten, one tablespoonful of lard or butter melted and three cups of sweet milk. Cook immediately on a hot griddle.

BREAD GRIDDLE-CAKES.

One quart of milk, boiling hot; two cups fine bread crumbs, three eggs, one tablespoonful melted butter, one-half teaspoonful salt, one-half teaspoonful soda dissolved in warm water; break the bread into the boiling milk, and let stand for ten minutes in a covered bowl, then beat to a smooth paste; add the yolks of the eggs well whipped, the butter, salt, soda, and finally the whites of the eggs previously whipped stiff, and add half of a cupful of flour. These can also be made of sour milk, soaking the bread in it over night and using a little more soda.

RICE GRIDDLE-CAKES.

Two cupfuls of cold boiled rice, one pint of flour, one teaspoonful sugar, one-half teaspoonful salt, one and one-half teaspoonfuls baking powder, one egg, a little more than half a pint of milk. Sift together flour, sugar, salt and powder; add rice free from lumps, diluted with beaten egg and milk; mix into smooth batter. Have griddle well heated, make cakes large, bake nicely brown, and serve with maple syrup.

POTATO GRIDDLE-CAKES.

Twelve large potatoes, three heaping tablespoonfuls of flour, one teaspoonful of baking powder, one-half teaspoonful salt, one or two eggs, two teacupfuls of boiling milk. The potatoes are peeled, washed and grated into a little cold water (which keeps them white), then strain off water and pour on boiling milk, stir in eggs, salt and flour, mixed with the baking powder; if agreeable, flavor with a little fine chopped onion; bake like any other pancakes, allowing a little more lard or butter. Serve with stewed or preserved fruit, especially with huckleberries.

GREEN CORN GRIDDLE-CAKES.

One pint of milk, two cups grated green corn, a little salt, two eggs, a teaspoonful of baking powder, flour sufficient to make a batter to fry on the griddle. Butter them hot and serve.

HUCKLEBERRY GRIDDLE-CAKES.

Made the same as above, leaving out one cup of milk, adding one tablespoonful of sugar and a pint of huckleberries rolled in flour. Blackberries or raspberries can be used in the same manner.

FRENCH GRIDDLE-CAKES.

Beat together until smooth six eggs and a pint sifted flour; melt one ounce of butter and add to the batter, with one ounce of sugar and a cup of milk; beat until smooth; put a tablespoonful at a time into a frying pan slightly greased, spreading the batter evenly over the surface by tipping the pan about; fry to a light brown; spread with jelly, roll up, dust with powdered sugar and serve hot.

RAISED BUCKWHEAT CAKES.

Take a small crock or large earthen pitcher, put into it a quart of warm water or half water and milk, one heaping teaspoonful of salt; then stir in as much buckwheat flour as will thicken it to rather a stiff batter; lastly, add half a cup of yeast; make it smooth, cover it up warm to rise over night; in the morning add a small, level teaspoonful of soda dissolved in a little warm water; this will remove any sour taste, if any, and increase the lightness.

Not a few object to eating buckwheat, as its tendency is to thicken the blood, and also to produce constipation; this can be remedied by making the batter one-third corn meal and two-thirds buckwheat, which makes the cakes equally as good. Many prefer them in this way.

BUCKWHEAT CAKES WITHOUT YEAST.

Two cups of buckwheat flour, one of wheat flour, a little salt, three teaspoonfuls baking powder; mix thoroughly and add about equal parts of milk and water until the batter is of the right consistency then stir until free from lumps. If they do not brown well, add a little molasses.

BUCKWHEAT CAKES.

Half a pint of buckwheat flour, a quarter of a pint of corn meal, a quarter of a pint of wheat flour, a little salt, two eggs beaten very light, one quart of new milk (made a little warm and mixed with the eggs before the flour is put in), one tablespoonful of butter or sweet lard, two large tablespoonfuls of yeast. Set it to rise at night for the morning. If in the least sour, stir in before baking just enough soda to correct the acidity. A very nice, but more expensive, recipe.

SWEDISH GRIDDLE-CAKES.

One pint of white flour, sifted; six eggs, whites and yolks beaten separately to the utmost; one saltspoonful of salt; one saltspoonful of soda dissolved in vinegar; milk to make a thin batter.

Beat the yolks light, add the salt, soda, two cupfuls of milk, then the flour and beaten whites alternately; thin with more milk if necessary.

CORN MEAL FRITTERS.

One pint of sour milk, one teaspoonful of salt, three eggs, one tablespoonful of molasses or sugar, one handful of flour, and corn meal enough to make a stiff batter; lastly, stir in a small teaspoonful of soda, dissolved in a little warm water.

This recipe is very nice made of rye flour.

CREAM FRITTERS.

One cup of cream, five eggs—the whites only, two full cups prepared flour, one saltspoonful of nutmeg, a pinch of salt. Stir the whites into the cream in turn with the flour, put in nutmeg and salt, beat all up hard for two minutes. The batter should be rather thick. Fry in plenty of hot, sweet lard, a spoonful of batter for each fritter. Drain, and serve upon a hot, clean napkin. Eat with jelly sauce. Pull, not cut, them open. Very nice.

CURRANT FRITTERS.

Two cupfuls dry, fine bread crumbs, two tablespoonfuls of prepared flour, two cups of milk, one-half pound currants, washed and well dried, five eggs whipped very light, one-half cup powdered sugar, one tablespoonful butter, one-half teaspoonful mixed cinnamon and nutmeg. Boil the milk and pour over the bread. Mix and put in the butter. Let it get cold. Beat in next the yolks and sugar, the seasoning, flour and stiff whites; finally, the currants dredged whitely with flour. The batter should be thick. Drop in great spoonfuls into the hot lard and fry. Drain them and send hot to table. Eat with a mixture of wine and powdered sugar.

WHEAT FRITTERS.

Three eggs, one and a half cups of milk, three teaspoonfuls baking powder, salt, and flour enough to make quite stiff, thicker than batter cakes. Drop into hot lard and fry like doughnuts.

A Good Sauce for the Above.—One cup of sugar, two tablespoonfuls of butter, one teaspoonful of flour beaten together; half a cup boiling water; flavor with extract lemon and boil until clear. Or serve with maple syrup.

APPLE FRITTERS.

Make a batter in the proportion of one cup sweet milk to two cups flour, a heaping teaspoonful of baking powder, two eggs beaten separately, one tablespoonful of sugar and a saltspoon of salt; heat the milk a little more than milk-warm, add it slowly to the beaten yolks and sugar; then add flour and whites of the eggs; stir all together and throw in thin slices of good sour apples, dipping the batter up over them; drop into boiling hot lard in large spoonfuls with pieces of apple in each, and fry to a light brown. Serve with maple syrup, or a nice syrup made with clarified sugar.

Bananas, peaches, sliced oranges and other fruits can be used in the same batter.

PINEAPPLE FRITTERS.

Make a batter as for apple fritters; then pare one large pineapple, cut it in slices a quarter of an inch thick, cut the slices in halves, dip them into the batter and fry them, and serve them as above.

PEACH FRITTERS.

Peel the peaches, split each in two and take out the stones; dust a little powdered sugar over them; dip each piece in the batter and fry in hot fat. A sauce to be served with them may be made as follows: Put an ounce of butter in a saucepan and whisk it to a cream; add four ounces of sugar gradually. Beat the yolks of two eggs; add to them a dash of nutmeg and a gill each of cold water and rum; stir this into the luke-warm batter and allow it to heat gradually. Stir constantly until of a smooth, creamy consistency, and serve. The batter is made as follows: Beat the yolks of three eggs; add to them a gill of milk, or half of a cupful, a saltspoonful of salt, four ounces of flour; mix. If old flour is used a little more milk may be found necessary.

GOLDEN-BALL FRITTERS.

Put into a stewpan a pint of water, a piece of butter as large as an egg and a tablespoonful of sugar. When it boils stir into it one pint of sifted flour, stirring briskly and thoroughly. Remove from the fire, and when nearly cooled beat into it six eggs, each one beaten separately and added one at a time, beating the batter between each. Drop the stiff dough into boiling lard by teaspoonfuls. Eat with syrup, or melted sugar and butter flavored.

Stirring the boiling lard around and around, so that it whirls when you drop in the fritters, causes them to assume a round shape like balls.

CANNELONS, OR FRIED PUFFS.

Half a pound of puff paste, apricot or any kind of preserve that may be preferred, hot lard.

Cannelons, which are made of puff paste rolled very thin, with jam enclosed, and cut out in long, narrow rolls or puffs, make a very pretty and elegant dish. Make some good puff paste, roll it out very thin, and cut it into pieces of an equal size, about two inches wide and eight inches long; place upon each piece a spoonful of jam, wet the edges with the white of egg and fold the paste over *twice*; slightly press the edges together, that the jam may not escape in the frying, and when all are prepared, fry them in boiling lard until of a nice brown, letting them remain by the side of the fire after they are colored, that the paste may be thoroughly done. Drain them before the fire, dish on a d'oyley, sprinkle over them sifted sugar and serve. These cannelons are very delicious made with fresh instead of preserved fruit, such as strawberries, raspberries or currants; they should be laid in the paste, plenty of pounded sugar sprinkled over and folded and fried in the same manner as stated above.

GERMAN FRITTERS.

Take slices of stale bread cut in rounds or stale cake; fry them in hot lard, like crullers, to a *light* brown. Dip each slice when fried in boiling milk, to remove the grease; drain quickly, dust with powdered sugar or spread with preserves. Pile on a hot plate and serve. Sweet wine sauce poured over them is very nice.

HOMINY FRITTERS.

Take one pint of hot boiled hominy, two eggs, half a teaspoonful of salt and a tablespoonful of flour; thin it a little with cold milk; when cold add a teaspoonful of baking powder, mix thoroughly, drop tablespoonfuls of it into hot fat and fry to a delicate brown.

PARSNIP FRITTERS.

Take three or four good-sized parsnips. Boil them until tender. Mash and season with a little butter, a pinch of salt and a slight sprinkling of pepper.

Have ready a plate with some sifted flour on it. Drop a tablespoonful of the parsnip in the flour and roll it about until well coated and formed into a ball. When you have a sufficient number ready, drop them into boiling drippings or lard, as you would a fritter; fry a delicate brown and serve hot. Do not put them in a covered dish, for that would steam them and deprive them of their crispness, which is one of their great charms.

These are also very good fried in a frying pan with a small quantity of lard and butter mixed, turning them over so as to fry both sides brown.

GREEN CORN FRITTERS.

One pint of grated, young and tender, green corn, three eggs, two tablespoonfuls of milk or cream, one tablespoonful of melted butter, if milk is used, a teaspoonful of salt. Beat the eggs well, add the corn by degrees, also the milk and butter; thicken with just enough flour to hold them together, adding a teaspoonful of baking powder to the flour. Have ready a kettle of hot lard, drop the corn from the spoon into the fat and fry a light brown. They are also nice fried in butter and lard mixed, the same as fried eggs.

CREAM SHORT-CAKE.

Sift one quart of fine white flour, rub into it three tablespoonfuls of cold butter, a teaspoonful of salt, a tablespoonful of white sugar. Add a beaten egg to a cup of sour cream, turn it into the other ingredients, dissolve a teaspoonful of soda in a spoonful of water, mix all together, handling as little as possible; roll lightly into two round sheets, place on pie-tins and bake from twenty to twenty-five minutes in a quick oven.

This crust is delicious for fruit short-cake.

STRAWBERRY SHORT-CAKE.

Make a rule of baking powder biscuit, with the exception of a little more shortening; divide the dough in half; lay one-half on the molding board (half the dough makes one short-cake), divide this half again, and roll each piece large enough to cover a biscuit-tin, or a large sized pie-tin; spread soft butter over the lower one and place the other on top of that; proceed with the other lump of dough the same, by cutting it in halves, and putting on another tin. Set them in the oven; when sufficiently baked take them out, separate each one by running a large knife through where the cold soft butter was spread. Then butter plentifully each crust, lay the bottom of each on earthen platters or dining-plates; cover thickly with a quart of strawberries that have been previously prepared with sugar, lay the top crusts on the fruit. If there is any juice left pour it around the cake. This makes a delicious short-cake.

Peaches, raspberries, blackberries and huckleberries can be substituted for strawberries. Always send to the table with a pitcher of sweet cream.

ORANGE SHORT-CAKE.

Peel two large oranges, chop them fine, remove the seeds, add half a peeled lemon and one cup of sugar. Spread between the layers of short-cake while it is hot.

ICING THE CAKES.

LEMON SHORT-CAKE.

Make a rich biscuit dough, same as above recipe. While baking, take a cup and a quarter of water, a cup and a half of sugar, and two lemons, peel, juice and pulp, throwing away the tough part of the rind; boil this for some little time; then stir in three crackers rolled fine; split the short-cakes while hot, spread with butter, then with the mixture. To be eaten warm.

HUCKLEBERRY SHORT-CAKE.

Two cupfuls of sugar, half a cupful of butter, one pint of sweet milk, one tablespoonful of salt, two heaping teaspoonfuls of baking powder sifted into a quart of flour, or enough to form a thick batter; add a quart of the huckleberries; to be baked in a dripper; cut into squares for the table and served hot with butter. Blackberries may be used the same.

FRIED DINNER-ROLLS.

When making light raised bread, save out a piece of dough nearly the size of a small loaf. Roll it out on the board, spread a tablespoonful of melted butter over it. Dissolve a quarter of a teaspoonful of soda in a tablespoonful of water and pour that also over it; work it all well into the dough, roll it out into a sheet not quite half an inch thick. Cut it in strips three inches long and one inch wide. Lay them on buttered tins, cover with a cloth and set away in a cool place until an hour before dinner time; then set them by the fire where they will become light. While they are rising, add to a frying-pan a tablespoonful of cold butter and one of lard; When it boils clear and is *hot*, lay as many of the rolls in as will fry nicely. As soon as they brown on one side turn them over and brown the other; then turn them on the edges and brown the sides. Add fresh grease as is needed. Eat them warm in place of bread. Nice with warm meat dinner.

NEWPORT BREAKFAST-CAKES.

Take one quart of dough from the bread at an early hour in the morning; break three eggs, separating yolks and whites, both to be whipped to a light froth; mix them into the dough and gradually add two tablespoonfuls of melted butter, one of sugar, one teaspoonful of soda, and enough warm milk with it until it is a batter the consistency of buckwheat cakes; beat it well and let it rise until breakfast time. Have the griddle hot and nicely greased, pour on the batter in small round cakes and bake a light brown, the same as any griddle cake.

PUFF BALLS.

To a piece of butter as large as an egg stirred until soft; add three well-beaten eggs, a pinch of salt and half a teacupful of sour cream. Stir well together, then add enough flour to make a very thick batter. Drop a spoonful of this into boiling water. Cook until the puffs rise to the surface. Dish them hot with melted butter turned over them. Nice accompaniment to a meat dinner as a side-dish—similar to plain macaroni.

BREAKFAST PUFFS.

Two cups of sour milk, one teaspoonful of soda, one teaspoonful of salt, one egg and flour enough to roll out like biscuit dough. Cut into narrow strips an inch wide and three inches long, fry brown in hot lard like doughnuts. Serve hot; excellent with coffee. Or fry in a spider with an ounce each of lard and butter, turning and browning all four of the sides.

ENGLISH CRUMPETS.

One quart of warm milk, half a cup of yeast, one teaspoonful of salt, flour enough to make a stiff batter; when light, add half a cupful of melted butter, a teaspoonful of soda dissolved in a little water and a very little more flour; let it stand twenty minutes or until light. Grease some muffin-rings, place them on a hot griddle and fill them half full of the batter; when done on one side turn and bake the other side. Butted them while hot; pile one on another and serve immediately.

PLAIN CRUMPETS.

Mix together thoroughly while dry one quart of sifted flour, loosely measured, two heaping teaspoonfuls baking powder and a little salt; then add two tablespoonfuls of melted butter and sweet milk enough to make a thin dough. Bake quickly in muffin-rings or patty-pans.

PREPARED BREAD CRUMBS.

Take pieces of stale bread, break them in small bits, put them on a baking pan and place them in a moderate oven, watching closely that they do not scorch; then take them while hot and crisp and roll them, crushing them. Sift them, using the fine crumbs for breading cutlets, fish, croquettes, etc. The coarse ones may be used for puddings, pancakes, etc.

CRACKERS.

Sift into a pint of flour a heaping teaspoonful of baking powder, four tablespoonfuls of melted butter, half a teaspoonful salt and the white of an egg beaten and one cup of milk; mix it with more flour, enough to make a very stiff dough, as stiff as can be rolled out; pounded and kneaded a long time. Roll very thin like pie crust and cut out either round or square. Bake a light brown.

Stale crackers are made crisp and better by placing them in the oven a few moments before they are needed for the table.

FRENCH CRACKERS.

Six eggs, twelve tablespoonfuls of sweet milk, six tablespoonfuls of butter, half a teaspoonful of soda; mold with flour, pounding and working half an hour; roll it thin. Bake with rather quick fire.

CORN MEAL MUSH OR HASTY PUDDING.

Put two quarts of water into a clean dinner-pot or stewpan, cover it and let it become boiling hot over the fire; then add a tablespoonful of salt, take off the light scum from the top, have sweet, fresh yellow or white corn meal; take a handful of the meal with the left hand and a pudding-stick in the right, then with the stick, stir the water around and by degrees let fall the meal; when one handful is exhausted, refill it; continue to stir and add meal until it is as thick as you can stir easily, or until the stick will stand in it; stir it awhile longer; let the fire be gentle; when it is sufficiently cooked, which will be in half an hour, it will bubble or puff up; turn it into a deep basin. This is eaten cold or hot, with milk or with butter and syrup or sugar, or with meat and gravy, the same as potatoes or rice.

FRIED MUSH.

Make it like the above recipe, turn it into bread tins and when cold slice it, dip each piece in flour and fry it in lard and butter mixed in the frying pan, turning to brown well both sides. Must be served hot.

GRAHAM MUSH.

Sift Graham meal slowly into boiling salted water, stirring briskly until thick as can be stirred with one hand; serve with milk or cream and sugar, or butter and syrup. It will be improved by removing from the kettle to a pan, as soon as thoroughly mixed, and steaming three or four hours. It may also be eaten cold, or sliced and fried, like corn meal mush.

OATMEAL.

Soak one cup of oatmeal in a quart of water over night, boil half an hour in the morning, salted to taste. It is better to cook it in a dish set into a dish of boiling water.

RICE CROQUETTES.

Boil for thirty minutes one cup of well-washed rice in a pint of milk; whip into the hot rice the following ingredients: Two ounces of butter, two ounces of sugar, some salt, and when slightly cool add the yolks of two eggs well beaten; if too stiff pour in a little more milk; when cold, roll into small balls and dip in beaten eggs, roll in fine cracker or bread crumbs, and fry same as doughnuts. Or they may be fried in the frying pan, with a tablespoonful each of butter and lard mixed, turning and frying both sides brown. Serve very hot.

HOMINY.

This form of cereal is very little known and consequently little appreciated in most Northern households. "Big hominy" and "little hominy," as they are called in the South, are staple dishes there and generally take the place of oatmeal, which is apt to be too heating for the climate. The former is called "samp" here. It must be boiled for at least eight hours to be properly cooked, and may then be kept on hand for two or three days and warmed over, made into croquettes or balls, or fried in cakes. The fine hominy takes two or three hours for proper cooking, and should be cooked in a dish set into another of boiling water, and kept steadily boiling until thoroughly soft.

HOMINY CROQUETTES.

To a cupful of cold boiled hominy, add a teaspoonful of melted butter, and stir it well, adding by degrees a cupful of milk, till all is made into a soft, light paste; add a teaspoonful of white sugar, a pinch of salt, and one well-beaten egg. Roll it into oval balls with floured hands, dipped in beaten egg, then rolled in cracker crumbs, and fry in hot lard.

The hominy is best boiled the day or morning before using.

BOILED RICE.

Take half or quarter of a pound of the best quality of rice; wash it in a strainer, and put it in a saucepan, with a quart of clean water and a pinch of salt; let it boil slowly till the water is all evaporated—see that it does not burn—then pour in a teacupful of new milk; stir carefully from the bottom of the saucepan, so that the upper grain may go under, but do not smash it; close the lid on your saucepan carefully down, and set it on a cooler part of the fire, where it will not boil; as soon as it has absorbed the added milk, serve it up with fresh new milk, adding fruit and sugar for those who like them.

Another nice way to cook rice is to take one teacupful of rice and one quart of milk, place in a steamer, and steam from two to three hours; when nearly done, stir in a piece of butter as large as the yolk of an egg, and a pinch of salt. You can use sugar if you like. The difference in the time of cooking depends on your rice—the older the rice, the longer it takes to cook.

SAMP, OR HULLED CORN.

An old-fashioned way of preparing hulled corn was to put a peck of old, dry, ripe corn into a pot filled with water, and with it a bag of hardwood ashes, say a quart. After soaking a while it was boiled until the skins or hulls came off easily. The corn was then washed in cold water to get rid of the taste of potash, and then boiled until the kernels were soft. Another way was to take the lye from the leaches where potash was made, dilute it, and boil the corn in this until the skins or hulls came off. It makes a delicious dish, eaten with milk or cream.

CRACKED WHEAT.

Soak the wheat over night in cold water, about a quart of water to a cup of wheat; cook it as directed for oatmeal; should be thoroughly done. Eaten with sugar and cream.

OAT FLAKES.

This healthful oat preparation may be procured from the leading grocers and is prepared as follows: Put into a double saucepan or porcelain-lined pan a quart of boiling water, add a saltspoonful of salt, and when it is boiling add, or rather stir in gradually, three ounces of flakes. Keep stirring to prevent burning. Let it boil from fifteen to twenty minutes and serve with cream and sugar.

Ordinarily oatmeal requires two hours' steady cooking to make it palatable and digestible. Wheaten grits and hominy one hour, but a half hour longer cooking will not injure them and makes them easier of digestion. Never be afraid of cooking cereals or preparations from cereals too long, no matter what the directions on the package may be.

STEAMED OATMEAL.

To one teacupful oatmeal add a quart of cold water, a teaspoonful of salt; put in a steamer over a kettle of cold water, gradually heat and steam an hour and a half after it begins to cook.

HOMINY.

Hominy is a preparation of Indian corn, broken or ground, either large or small, and is an excellent breakfast dish in winter or summer. Wash the hominy thoroughly in on 3 or two waters, then cover it with twice its depth of cold water and let it come to a boil slowly. If it be the large hominy, simmer six hours; if the small hominy, simmer two hours. When the water evaporates add hot water; when done it may be eaten with cream, or allowed to become cold and warmed up in the frying pan, using a little butter to prevent burning.

TOAST.

Toast should be made of stale bread, or at least of bread that has been baked a day. Cut smoothly in slices, not more than half an inch thick; if the crust is baked very hard, trim the edges and brown very evenly, but if it happens to burn, that should be scraped off. Toast that is to be served with anything turned over it, should have the slices first dipped quickly in a dish of hot water turned from the boiling tea-kettle, with a little salt thrown in. Cold biscuits cut in halves, and the under crust sliced off, then browned evenly on both sides, make equally as good toast. The following preparations of toast are almost all of them very nice dishes, served with a family breakfast.

MILK TOAST.

Put over the fire a quart of milk, put into it a tablespoonful of cold butter, stir a heaping teaspoonful of flour into half a gill of milk; as soon as the milk on the fire boils, stir in the flour, add a teaspoonful of salt; let all boil up once, remove from the fire, and dip in this slices of toasted bread. When all are used up, pour what is left of the scalded milk over the toast. Cover and send to the table hot.

CREAM TOAST.

Heat a pint of milk to boiling and add a piece of butter the size of an egg; stir a tablespoonful of flour smoothly into a cup of rich cream, and add some of the boiling milk to this; heat it gradually and prevent the flour from lumping; then stir into the boiling milk and let it cook a few moments; salt to taste. After taking from the fire stir in a beaten egg; strain the mixture on to toast lightly buttered.

AMERICAN TOAST.

To one egg thoroughly beaten, put one cup of sweet milk and a little salt. Slice light bread and dip into the mixture, allowing each slice to absorb some of the milk; then brown on a hot buttered griddle or thick-bottomed frying pan; spread with butter and serve hot.

NUNS' TOAST.

Cut four or five hard-boiled eggs into slices. Put a piece of butter half the size of an egg into a saucepan and when it begins to bubble add a finely chopped onion. Let the onion cook a little without taking color, then stir in a teaspoonful of flour. Add a cupful of milk and stir until it becomes smooth; then put in the slices of eggs and let them get hot. Pour over neatly trimmed slices of hot buttered toast. The sauce must be seasoned to taste with pepper and salt.

CHEESE TOAST. No. 1.

Toast thin slices of bread an even, crisp brown. Place on a warm plate, allowing one small slice to each person, and pour on enough melted cheese to cover them. Rich new cheese is best. Serve while warm. Many prefer a little prepared mustard spread over the toast before putting on the cheese.

CHEESE TOAST. No. 2.

Put half an ounce of butter in a frying pan; when hot add gradually four ounces of mild American cheese. Whisk it thoroughly until melted. Beat together half a pint of cream and two eggs; whisk into the cheese, add a little salt, pour over the crisp toast, and serve.

The two above recipes are usually called "Welsh Rarebit."

OYSTER TOAST.

Select the large ones, used for frying, and first dip them in beaten egg, then in either cracker or bread crumbs and cook upon a fine wire gridiron, over a quick fire. Toast should be made ready in advance, and a rich cream sauce poured over the whole. After pouring on the sauce, finely cut celery strewn over the top adds to their delicacy.

Or wash oysters in the shell and put them on hot coals, or upon the top of a hot stove, or bake them in a hot oven; open the shells with an oyster-knife, taking care to lose none of the liquor. Dip the toast into hot, salted water quickly and turn out the oyster and liquor over the toast; season with salt and pepper and a teaspoonful of melted butter over each.

Oysters steamed in the shell are equally as good.

MUSHROOMS ON TOAST.

Peel a quart of mushrooms and cut off a little of the root end. Melt an ounce of butter in the frying pan and fry in it half a pound of raw minced steak; add two saltspoonfuls of salt, a pinch of cayenne and a gill of hot water; fry until the juices are extracted from the meat; tilt the pan and squeeze the meat with the back of the spoon until there is nothing left but dry meat, then remove it; add the mushrooms to the liquid and if there is not enough of it, add more butter; toss them about a moment and pour out on hot toast.

Some add a little sherry to the dish before removing from the fire.

TOMATO TOAST.

Pare and stew a quart of ripe tomatoes until smooth. Season with salt, pepper and a tablespoonful of butter. When done, add one cup sweet cream and a little flour. Let it scald, but not boil; remove at once. Pour over slices of dipped toast, well buttered.

EGGS ON TOAST.

Various preparations of eggs can be served on toast, first dipping slices of well-toasted bread quickly in hot salted water, then turning over them scrambled, poached or creamed eggs, all found in the recipes among EGGS.

BAKED EGGS ON TOAST.

Toast six slices of stale bread, dip them in hot salted water and butter them lightly. After arranging them on a platter or deep plate, break enough eggs to cover them, breaking one at a time and slip over the toast so that they do not break; sprinkle over them salt and pepper and turn over all some kind of thickened gravy—either chicken or lamb, cream or a cream sauce made the same as "White Sauce;" turn this over the toast and eggs and bake in a hot oven until the eggs are set, or about five minutes. Serve at once.

HAM TOAST.

Take a quarter of a pound of either boiled or fried ham, chop it fine, mix it with the yolks of two eggs, well beaten, a tablespoonful of butter, and enough cream or rich milk to make it soft, a dash of pepper. Stir it over the fire until it thickens. Dip the toast for an instant in hot salted water; spread over some melted butter, then turn over the ham mixture. Serve hot.

REED BIRDS ON TOAST.

Remove the feathers and legs of a dozen reed birds, split them down the back, remove the entrails, and place them on a double broiler; brush a little melted butter over them and broil the inner side thoroughly first; then lightly broil the other side. Melt one quarter of a pound of butter, season it nicely with salt and pepper, dip the birds in it, and arrange them nicely on slices of toast.

MINCED FOWLS ON TOAST.

Remove from the bones all the meat of either cold roast or boiled fowls. Clean it from the skin, and keep covered from the air until ready for use. Boil the bones and skin with three-fourths of a pint of water until reduced quite half. Strain the gravy and let it cool. Next, having skimmed off the fat, put it into a clean saucepan with half a cup of cream, three tablespoonfuls of butter, well mixed with a tablespoonful of flour. Keep these stirred until they boil. Then put in the fowl finely minced, with three hard-boiled eggs, chopped, and sufficient salt and pepper to season. Shake the mince over the fire until just ready to serve. Dish it over hot toast and serve.

HASHED BEEF ON TOAST.

Chop a quantity of cold roast beef rather fine and season it well with pepper and salt. For each pint of meat add a level tablespoonful of flour. Stir well and add a small teacupful of soup-stock or water. Put the mixture into a small stewpan and, after covering it, simmer for twenty minutes. Meanwhile, toast half a dozen slices of bread nicely and at the end of the twenty minutes spread the meat upon them. Serve at once on a hot dish. In case water be used instead of soup-stock, add a tablespoonful of butter just before spreading the beef upon the toast. Any kind of cold meat may be prepared in a similar manner.

Maria Parloa.

VEAL HASH ON TOAST.

Take a teacupful of boiling water in a saucepan, stir in an even teaspoonful of flour, wet in a tablespoonful of cold water, and let it boil five minutes; add one-half teaspoonful of black pepper, as much salt and two tablespoonfuls of butter, and let it keep hot, but not boil. Chop the veal fine and mix with it half as much stale bread crumbs. Put it in a pan and pour the gravy over it, then let it simmer ten minutes. Serve this on buttered toast.

CODFISH ON TOAST. (Cuban Style.)

Take a teacupful of freshened codfish picked up fine. Fry a sliced onion in a tablespoonful of butter; when it has turned a light brown, put in the fish with water enough to cover it; add half a can of tomatoes, or half a dozen of fresh ones. Cook all nearly an hour, seasoning with a little pepper. Serve on slices of dipped toast, hot. Very fine.

Plain creamed codfish is very nice turned over dipped toast.

HALIBUT ON TOAST.

Put into boiling salted water one pound of fresh halibut; cook slowly for fifteen minutes, or until done; remove from the water and chop it fine; then add half a cup of melted butter and eight eggs well beaten. Season with salt and pepper.

Place over the fire a thick-bottomed frying pan containing a tablespoonful of cold butter; when it begins to melt, tip the pan so as to grease the sides; then put in the fish and eggs and stir one way until the eggs are cooked, but not *too* hard. Turn over toast dipped in hot salted water.

CHICKEN HASH WITH RICE TOAST.

Boil a cup of rice the night before; put it into a square, narrow bread-pan, set it in the ice-box. Next morning cut it in half inch slices, rub over each slice a little warm butter and toast them on a broiler to a delicate brown. Arrange the toast on a warm platter and turn over the whole a chicken hash made from the remains of cold fowl, the meat picked from the bones, chopped fine, put into the frying pan with butter and a little water to moisten it, adding pepper and salt. Heat hot all through. Serve immediately.

APPLE TOAST.

Cut six apples into quarters, take the core out, peel and cut them in slices; put in the saucepan an ounce of butter, then throw over the apples about two ounces of white powdered sugar and two tablespoonfuls of water; put the saucepan on the fire, let it stew quickly, toss them up, or stir with a spoon; a few minutes will do them. When tender cut two or three slices of bread half an inch thick; put in a frying pan two ounces of butter, put on the fire; when the butter is melted put in your bread, which fry of a nice yellowish color; when nice and crisp take them out, place them on a dish, a little white sugar over, the apples about an inch thick. Serve hot.